SEMINAR STUDIES IN HISTORY

Editor: Patrick Richardson

HENRY VII

SEMINAR STUDIES IN HISTORY

Editor: Patrick Richardson

A full list of titles in this
series will be found on the
back cover of this book

SEMINAR STUDIES IN HISTORY

HENRY VII

Roger Lockyer

Lecturer in History
Royal Holloway College
University of London

LONGMAN

LONGMAN GROUP LIMITED
London

Associated companies, branches and representatives
throughout the world

© Longman Group Ltd (formerly
Longmans, Green & Co Ltd) 1968

First published 1968
Third impression 1972

ISBN 0 582 31386 4

Printed in Malta by St Paul's Press Ltd

Contents

INTRODUCTION TO THE SERIES   vii

Part One · Background

1 SOCIAL AND ECONOMIC BACKGROUND   3

Changes in Towns and Countryside   3
Magnates and Gentry   5
The Machinery of Government   7
The Weakness of the Crown   9

2 THE YORKIST INHERITANCE   11

The Council   11
Financial Administration   14

Part Two · Analysis

3 FINANCE   19

The New King   19
Exchequer and Chamber   22
Feudal and Prerogative Revenue   25
The Problem of Coordination   28
Henry's Achievement   31

4 ADMINISTRATION   32

The Council   32
The Council Learned   34
The Common Law   37
The Council in Star Chamber   38
Other Councils   41
Justices of the Peace   44

5 PARLIAMENT   48

The Lords   48
The Commons   49
The Functions of Parliament: 1. Money Grants   53
The Functions of Parliament: 2. Statute Law   57

6 THE ECONOMY   64

Enclosures   64
Wool and Cloth   67
The Expansion of Overseas Trade   71
The Encouragement of English Shipping   75

7 FOREIGN POLICY (INCLUDING IRELAND, SCOTLAND AND
THE PRETENDERS)   78

The States of Western Europe   78
Ireland   80
Brittany   82
Perkin Warbeck   84
The Closing Years of the Reign   88

Part Three · Assessment

8 CONCLUSION   97

Part Four · Documents

Documents   105

Appendices

Chronological Summary   147

Generalogies   150

Bibliography   154

Index   158

Introduction to the Series

The seminar method of teaching is being used increasingly in VI forms and at universities. It is a way of learning in smaller groups through discussion, designed both to get away from and to supplement the basic lecture techniques. To be successful, the members of a seminar must be informed, or else—in the unkind phrase of a cynic, it can be a 'pooling of ignorance'. The chapter in the textbook of English or European history by its nature cannot provide material in this depth, but at the same time the full academic work may be too long and perhaps too advanced for students at this level.

For this reason we have invited practising teachers in universities, schools and colleges of further education to contribute short studies on specialised aspects of British and European history with these special needs and pupils of this age in mind. For this series the authors have been asked to provide, in addition to their basic analysis, a full selection of documentary material of all kinds and an up-to-date and comprehensive bibliography. Both these sections are referred to in the text, but it is hoped that they will prove to be valuable teaching and learning aids in themselves.

Note on the System of References:

A bold number in round brackets (**5**) in the text refers the reader to the corresponding entry in the Bibliography section at the end of the book.

A bold number in square brackets, preceded by 'doc.' [**docs 6, 8**] refers the reader to the corresponding items in the section of Documents, which follows the main text.

PATRICK RICHARDSON
General Editor

Part One

BACKGROUND

1 Social and Economic Background

CHANGES IN TOWNS AND COUNTRYSIDE

The fifteenth century is often thought of as an inglorious epilogue to the Middle Ages—a period of shrinking populations, economic recession, and the break-up of established patterns of life and thought in a welter of bloodshed. In England, according to this interpretation, the process of decay came to its climax in the Wars of the Roses when an unprincipled nobility plunged the country into chaos in the selfish pursuit of profit and power, only to leave itself exhausted and the way open for the rise of a new monarchy and a new society.

Such a picture is not, of course, without its elements of truth, but the colours are too vivid, the generalisations too sweeping. In the first place the fifteenth century was not a coherent whole—what is true of one part of it is false of another; and secondly, many of its worst features had been common to English and European society for a long period beforehand, and were to continue well beyond its close. Warfare and turbulence were admittedly endemic, but these were facts of human nature rather than characteristics of the period 1400–1500; and while it is true that some areas and some occupations were, economically, in decline, it is equally true that for others the period was one of advancement and prosperity.

From about 1450 onwards the population, which had shrunk to some two million, began slowly to increase, thereby creating both an expanding market and an expanding labour force—the pre-requisites of a buoyant economy. This population was, moreover, a mobile one, and if the picture of medieval England as a static society—in which succeeding generations lived out their lives on the same plot of land, rarely venturing beyond the horizon—ever had any truth, it certainly does not apply to this period. Everywhere there was movement and change. This was particularly marked in areas like East Anglia, the west country, and the West Riding of

Yorkshire, where the cloth industry was establishing itself outside the corporate towns with their restrictive regulations. While villages like Lavenham were becoming industrial centres, some of the older towns were in decay. Coventry, for instance, which boasted a population of 10,000 at the time of the Black Death, had less than 7,000 in 1520, and during the same period the population of York shrank from 14,000 to 8,000. But other towns were booming. Southampton, with the advantage of its magnificent natural harbour, was becoming one of the main centres for trade with Italy; and London, the commercial as well as the political capital of the country, was continually expanding, and had some 50,000 inhabitants by the time Henry VII came to the throne.

The prosperity of foreign trade and domestic industry was based on wool, and the demand for this brought about big changes in the countryside. In the midland area in particular the depopulation of villages and hamlets was widespread. Sheep needed few men to look after them and brought in a rich reward, and landowners were obviously tempted to make a quick profit where they could do so by evicting peasants, pulling down their hovels, and turning the land over to pasture. Complaints of depopulating enclosures and deserted villages do not become commonplace until the Tudor period, but in fact the greatest damage had already been done by the time Bosworth was fought.

While some peasants were evicted and turned out on to the roads, others prospered. The 'classical' type of manor, in which nearly all the tenants were dependent and held their lands in return for compulsory labour services on their lord's demesne, was no longer the prevailing pattern (in some parts of the country, of course, it never had been). The labour shortage resulting from the Black Death had been a blessing for the serfs, who could hope now to strike a bargain with their landlord instead of merely accepting an hereditary servile status. Dependent tenures were gradually being replaced by copyhold and leasehold, and villeinage was on its way out. The owners of the land were no longer concerned to cultivate it themselves: it was easier for them to lease the demesne to a prosperous peasant. Consequently the pattern of rural society became much more intricate. Laziness, illness, or bad luck could keep a man down near subsistence level; but those peasants who were prepared to work hard, and who had luck on their side, could push their children, if not themselves, into a much higher level of society. Clement Paston, for instance, who died in 1419, had only a small farm in Norfolk and married a villein, but he sent his son William to Eton, even though he had to borrow money to do so. William became a distinguished lawyer, was appointed Justice of the Common Pleas, and married into a gentry family. The third generation of Pastons were gentry born, and carried out the obligations expected of them as knights of the shire and justices of the peace.

MAGNATES AND GENTRY

With the breakdown of the manorial society and economy, a new basis had to be found for the obligations that bind a community together and stop it from fragmenting into anarchy. Such a basis depended, inevitably, on the territorial magnates, whose power was so great that any system which ignored them would have had no chance of operating. Magnate influence had been, of course, a characteristic of medieval feudal society, but in that earlier period there was a much closer correlation between the land a man held and the obligations or rights that he had. In the bastard feudalism that developed from the late thirteenth century onwards, money and other pressures could extend a lord's influence far beyond the territories he actually possessed, and a whole network of obligations could be built up, not easy to define and constantly changing, yet nonetheless a political fact of the first importance.

Bastard feudalism has had a bad press and has been blamed for much of the turmoil of the fifteenth century. Yet it was as much a symptom as a cause of the breakdown of royal authority, and although it led frequently to disorder it was also a means of order. Magnates were expected to look after those who wore their livery or who were dependent upon them in less obvious ways, and although their protection might take illegal forms—such as bribing a sheriff or intimidating a jury—it did provide some sort of stability. The older loyalties, bound up so closely with land, tended to be narrow and sectional. For the national states that were emerging in western Europe a broader concept of loyalty was necessary, ultimately focusing upon the person of the sovereign. Bastard feudalism was, however unconsciously, a means to this end.

In the short run, of course, the justification of bastard feudalism lies in the fact that it sprang from the political realities of the situation. In the absence of effective royal, central authority the magnates were the natural leaders of society, and the abuse of power by individual magnates was probably no more typical of the fifteenth than of any earlier century. The more powerful the magnates became the more they impeded the chances of a restoration of central authority, but meanwhile, in the absence of such authority, the rule of the strong was better than no rule at all.

The great magnates were not, in any case, all uncivilised brutes, interested only in fighting. Admittedly they were often quick-tempered, unscrupulous, adept at political intrigue and ready to resort to violence where litigation failed. But such characteristics were not necessarily incompatible with a love of the arts and learning. Humphrey, Duke of Gloucester, a brother and companion-in-arms of Henry V, was a generous patron of men of letters and left his considerable library to Oxford University; while his brother, the Duke of Bedford, who spent most of his time fighting in France, gave money to the university to endow lectureships. Later in the century John Tiptoft, Earl of Worcester, who married the King-maker's sister and, as Constable of England, earned a reputation for butchering his political opponents, was also renowned as a Latin scholar of considerable ability, who translated Cicero into English and was eulogised by Caxton for his patronage of learning.

While the break-up of the older type of manorial feudalism created the conditions in which the greater magnates could enormously extend their range of influence, it also made society more fluid, and gave an opportunity for the lesser landowners (ranging from gentry to peasant-freeholders), wealthy townsmen and professional men, particularly lawyers, to play a more important part in social and political life. Their prosperity would usually depend—as with the Pastons—upon becoming the clients of one of the magnates, and their fortunes might vary with those of their patron, but by skilful playing-off of one magnate against another they could maintain a degree of independence. The smaller land-owners acted as sheriffs, justices of the peace and escheators, and because these offices were no threat to magnate power they kept their importance. The very fact that the magnates could control the key posts in local and central government encouraged them to preserve the existing structure. Therefore, beneath the surface of aristocratic rule, another section of society was taking over the operation of the mechanism of government. This mechanism worked in favour of the magnates, but given a strong royal initiative it could once again be made to reinforce the authority of the crown. The mechanism as such was neutral; it was there to be operated by whoever was powerful enough to do so.

THE MACHINERY OF GOVERNMENT

The paradox of magnate power was shown clearly in central government. During the fifteenth century the House of Commons acquired a prestige it had not had before. Its assent became indispensable to legislation, and its petitions formed the basis for many of the statutes of the period. In some ways this appearance of power was misleading, since the magnates exerted considerable influence in the election of members and in the framing of petitions. But in parliament, as in the localities, the fact that the magnates chose to work through the existing system encouraged the system to develop. The Commons might appear more powerful than in fact they were; they were indisputably more powerful than they had previously been. As the Tudors were later to discover, an institution, which, because it is apparently easily controllable, is encouraged to assert itself, rapidly develops a genuine authority and independence which transform its position. This changing position was reflected in the personnel of the Commons. Representation was no longer regarded as a burden. Boroughs sought a charter giving them the right to elect a member, and individuals were eager to be elected. The invasion of borough seats by the local gentry, which was to reach its climax in the sixteenth century, had already begun in the fifteenth, and the House of Commons was drawn from the same group— gentry, prosperous freeholders, richer merchants and lawyers— which was establishing itself in local life. Here, once again, magnate rule was a shelter under which smaller men could not merely take refuge but also put down foundations and build.

The period of magnate predominance saw no breakdown in the machinery of central government. If this had proved a real obstacle to aristocratic ambitions it would no doubt have been cast aside, and England might have become little more than a geographical term embracing autonomous principalities. But because the magnates made it their highest ambition to take over the government of the whole country, it was obviously to their advantage to keep the machinery of government in existence, particularly as they could use it, where necessary, for their own short-term ends. The Council, for instance, remained the heart of government, and was dominated by the magnates, who claimed, as peers, a 'natural right' to formulate policy. The great offices of state similarly came under magnate control, and for this reason continued to operate. The Exchequer, for example, functioned throughout the reign of Henry VI, and the law courts at Westminster sat undisturbed throughout the worst days of the civil wars. The effectiveness of these organs of government was, of course, impaired by the conditions of fifteenth century society—since decisions made at Westminster would depend for their enforcement upon the cooperation of sheriffs and justices of the peace, who would be unlikely to carry them out except with the approval of their aristocratic patrons—but the machinery survived and went through the motions. Edward IV and Henry VII were not given the opportunity, even had they wished it, of building the state anew: all they had to do was to make the existing system function efficiently.

The ineffectiveness of central authority, the spread of bastard feudalism, the breakdown of order and the frequent outbursts of private war, all these were results, as well as causes, of the weakness of the crown. The medieval English monarchy had been strong— one of the strongest in Europe—and had developed organs of government which were sophisticated, responsive to changing needs and conditions, and able in routine matters to operate independently of the king. But in the last resort the effectiveness of government depended on the effectiveness of the king, and it was failure at the centre that led to the collapse of the medieval monarchy. The long war against France, which occupied most of the fourteenth century, put an intolerable strain on royal finances, and the king became increasingly dependent upon the magnates not only for money but also for the men to fight in his armies. The feudal levy was not a flexible enough instrument for prolonged campaigns; indentured retainers were far more effective, but these were virtually private armies belonging to mighty subjects.

THE WEAKNESS OF THE CROWN

Richard II, who found his freedom of action limited by shortage of money and the growth of magnate power—unwelcome inheritances from his grandfather Edward III—tried to develop his prerogative rights and to check the tendency towards oligarchy by creating an autocracy. His attempt failed, because the crown could not survive in isolation and there was no group other than the magnates to which he could turn. His failure was symbolised by his deposition in 1399 and the accession of a man who was himself a magnate, the Duke of Lancaster. The new king, Henry IV, had the advantage of magnate support, but only on condition that he reversed the tendencies of his predecessor's policy and tried to work with the leaders of the aristocracy instead of against them. The authority of the crown consequently diminished, and although Henry V, who succeeded his father in 1413, sent its prestige soaring by reopening the Hundred Years War, the cost was enormous and made the crown increasingly dependent on both individual magnates and the parliament which they controlled.

Henry V's early death in 1422 was a disaster, for his son was a minor, and the great nobles who surrounded him, and who were connected by blood with the crown, could hardly be expected to sit still and wait for him to grow up. Ambition spurred them on, and also fear—the fear that if they did not act they might be overthrown by others more ruthless. There was also this to be said for the great magnates—the Percies, the Nevilles, the de la Poles, and their peers; they had experience of government on their own estates, which were, in effect, petty kingdoms with their own chanceries, exchequers and administrative officers. The magnates were also sufficiently free from material cares to be able to devote their time to political life. They had only to look around them to see that poverty and personal incapacity were destroying the effectiveness of the monarchy. By the time Henry VI came of age order might well have given way to anarchy; and what if he proved to be a weakling? Henry VI was, after all, only the grandson of the magnate Duke of Lancaster, who had claimed the throne for himself. Why should not another magnate restore order by wresting the crown from the now enfeebled hands of Lancaster? This was the reasoning that led Richard of York to make his famous claim in 1460.

The struggle between York and Lancaster, in which the leading magnates were all, inevitably, involved, marks the lowest point in the fortunes of the medieval monarchy. The degree and duration of disorder should not be exaggerated. One historian has estimated that the total period of active campaigning between the first battle, at St Albans in 1455, and the last battle, at Stoke in 1487, amounted to twelve or thirteen weeks at most, in a period of thirty-two years (**8,** pp. 20–1). The armies involved were small; no English towns were sacked or even besieged for any length of time; and the amount of damage inflicted was insignificant compared with what the English themselves had done in France. Throughout the greater part of the country life continued much as usual, and although the poverty of the crown put a brake on royal building, the masons were hard at work on parish and monastic churches. Even the fortified houses that were built during this period were designed far more for comfort than defence.

Yet even though the civil war was limited in its impact, it accelerated the impulse towards disorder that was already affecting English society. Had it gone on indefinitely it would have given England the characteristics once thought to be typical of South American republics—anarchy punctuated by revolution—and would have consumed the energies that were to be used so creatively in Tudor England. The only possible outcome, other than stalemate, was the triumph of one of the magnates and the restoration of royal authority. This happened in March 1461, when Edward, Duke of York, destroyed the Lancastrian army at Towton. Just over a year later he was crowned king as Edward IV.

The accession of Edward IV was not the end of the civil war, but it was the beginning of the end. The reforms which he set on foot were elaborated under his successors, Richard III and Henry VII, and the revival of royal power, which he began, increased in pace, despite interruptions, until it brought the wars finally to a close and established in England a monarchy more powerful than anything that had existed since the days of Edward I. But if Edward IV inherited bloodshed and anarchy, he also inherited the structure of the medieval state and its organs of government. The magnates, weakened by war, were no longer an insuperable barrier to the exercise of central authority, and Edward unlike Richard II, could appeal for the support of another important section of the community, already trained in law and administration and ready to serve any monarch who would give them the ordered and stable society in which they could flourish.

2 The Yorkist Inheritance

Edward IV was under twenty when he became king, and the energy which his strong physique gave him was reinforced by his determination to be an effective ruler. He had many of the qualities needed for success (**54**). He won men to him by his charm and easy manners, while women found his good looks irresistible, but he was no mere playboy. He could be ruthless in the pursuit of his aims, even when this meant executing his own brother, and he had a keen business sense. Poverty and lack of will had enfeebled royal government; Edward was well qualified to remedy both. He brought to the crown the considerable possessions of the Duchy of York, including the Mortimer inheritance; he confiscated the Duchy of Lancaster; he resumed by Act of parliament those lands which had been allowed to slip out of royal control; and by acts of attainder he transferred to himself the lands of many of his enemies.

THE COUNCIL

The king's determination to rule had an immediate impact upon the Council. Under Henry VI this had become a semi-independent body, dominated by the magnates, and Fortescue accurately summarised its weaknesses. 'The king's Council was wont to be chosen of great princes, and of the greatest lords of the land, both spiritual and temporal and also of other men that were in great authority and offices. Which lords and officers had at hand also many matters of their own to be treated in the Council, as had the king. Where through, when they came together, they were so occupied with their own matters and with the matters of their kin, servants and tenants, that they attended but little, and other while nothing, to the king's matters' (**7**, p. 145). Many of the Council's records have been lost, and until fairly recently it was assumed that the Council as such disappeared with the accession of Edward IV.

11

Recent research has clearly demonstrated, however, that only the old type of magnate-dominated Council disappeared (**55, 56**). Edward's rule was more personal than that of his immediate predecessors, but like any king he needed advisers, and the work of the Council can be traced in the administrative, and particularly the financial, policies of the reign.

For the period 1461–70 the names have survived of 124 people who were called 'councillors' and who presumably took a special oath to the king. Eighty-eight of these were councillors in the second part of the reign, after Edward's restoration in 1471, and they were made up as follows: twenty-one nobles, thirty-five ecclesiastics, twenty-three household officials, and nine others. These proportions tell us a considerable amount about Edward's methods. They show, for instance, that he did not make any deliberate attempt to exclude the nobles from his Council: to do so would, in any case, have been foolhardy, since the nobles were still the most powerful men in the localities where they lived, and provided they were prepared to cooperate their loyalty could be of enormous help to the crown. The ecclesiastics played a major part because they were literate, because they could be rewarded for service to the state by promotion in the church, and because they had no legitimate heirs who could inherit their estates and turn a personal duty to give advice into an hereditary right to be consulted. Most significant is the group of household officials, which had doubled in numbers compared with the first half of the reign. These were drawn from the second rank of English society, the lawyers and estate-administrators who were already occupying many of the key positions in local government, and who assumed the leadership of local life once the magnate stranglehold had been broken. The nobles might still hold the great offices, with all their honours and dignities, but effective power went to these officials whose range of authority expanded with that of the crown.

The actual number of councillors present at any meeting fluctuated considerably, twenty being the highest attendance recorded in the surviving documents. The king summoned whom he liked when he liked, and although he presumably had several intimate advisers whose opinion he particularly trusted, nobody could claim the *right* to be present. As far as policy-making was concerned, the role of the Council was purely advisory. It would, at the king's invitation, discuss matters and recommend certain lines of action, but Edward was free to accept or reject these as he pleased. The magnate-Council of the late-Lancastrian period had issued its own directives, authenticating them with the Privy Seal, but under Edward the king's personal seal, or signet, became increasingly important. The signet could be used to prompt the Privy Seal to action, or to issue orders direct, and the greater volume of business reflected on the position of the king's secretary. This position was held, under Edward IV, by William Hatteclyffe, and the fact that he handled the king's correspondence made him, at a time when royal power was staging such a marked recovery, a man of influence and importance. But his main concern was still with diplomacy and foreign affairs, and although the secretaryship was at the beginning of that development which was to make it, in the Tudor period, one of the most important offices of state, it remained of secondary political significance under Edward IV.

No amount of conciliar activity would have been of any use if it had been disregarded in the localities. The big problem of Edward's reign was to make the royal will effective throughout the country as a whole, and this meant making sure that sheriffs, justices of the peace and borough corporations obeyed the king's commands. There was no short cut to such a situation. It meant keeping up a steady pressure—issuing orders, insisting upon compliance, summoning offenders to appear before the Council, and so on. Had all the local officials refused to obey, Edward would have been powerless, since he had no police force or standing army. But in fact there was a widespread wish to cooperate, particularly among the gentry, merchants and lawyers who controlled local life in the absence of any overmighty subject.

The civil war had done much to cut down the power of such overmighty subjects. Many of the more prominent ones had been killed, often leaving their estates in the hands of minors, and all had been weakened by the financial strain of maintaining private armies. There were still powerful aristocrats, and corruption and bullying remained features of local life; but many nobles welcomed Edward's accession, and the Lancastrian leaders who found him unacceptable were in exile or lying low. Edward deliberately encouraged aristocratic influence where it could serve his purposes. He presented Lord Hastings, for instance, with large grants from confiscated property in the Midlands; he gave William Herbert lands and offices to increase his power in Wales; and he released Henry Percy from the

Tower so that he could restore order in the north and counteract the Neville influence there.

There was nothing new about Edward's methods of restoring order, except the vigour which he put into the administration. The judges, the common law, the Council, the justices of peace and the sheriffs—these were long-established and were the only means he had available. His success came from the fact that he made these instruments work, and used his own authority to reinforce that of local officials who were liable to be brow-beaten. In 1475, for example, when the end of the French campaign led to unrest and violence from demobilised soldiers, Edward went in person to some of the more disturbed areas, demonstrating by his presence his determination to be obeyed.

FINANCIAL ADMINISTRATION

The weakness of royal government had sprung, in large part, from shortage of money, and Edward realised that by making the crown rich again he would go a long way to restoring its authority. Parliamentary grants might have been one way of acquiring riches, but Edward knew that these aroused a great deal of opposition and merely added to the disorder he was trying to eradicate. Parliament, in any case, had been a focus for opposition to the crown during the Lancastrian period, and Edward may well have thought that a break with the past would imply a reduction in the role of parliament. He was not anti-parliamentary—he summoned six parliaments during a reign of twenty-two years—but, as he told the Commons in 1467, 'I purpose to live upon my own, and not to charge my subjects but in great and urgent causes concerning the weal of themselves and also the defence of them and of this my realm, rather than my own pleasure'.

If Edward was to 'live of his own' he would have to exploit to the full the sources of income available to him. The medieval monarchy had developed, in the Exchequer, a sophisticated and elaborate mechanism for collecting and auditing the king's revenues, but its procedure was slow and during the civil wars it had fallen badly into arrears. Also the elaborate checks and counterchecks for which the Exchequer was famous made it less suitable for Edward's purposes. He wanted to exercise the same close, personal control over his revenues that he exercised over policy-making, and for this purpose he developed the Chamber. The Exchequer was not destroyed, but it was increasingly by-passed. It was too understaffed and too inflexible to deal with an expanding revenue, and Edward's income expanded rapidly. He did not have to make lavish grants of royal lands to a greedy aristocracy, nor did he have to squander his income on fighting the French; when to these negative factors were added the positive ones of additional lands acquired through attainders, and more efficient exploitation of existing revenues, the need for the Chamber becomes apparent.

From the beginning of his reign Edward ordered that certain moneys should be paid direct to the Chamber and not into the Exchequer, but the auditing of these accounts was still done by the Exchequer. Later on, however, Edward—following the example of the Duchy of Lancaster, which was regarded as a model of what efficient estate administration ought to be—appointed special auditors to deal with the accounts of newly acquired lands. Although these 'foreign' auditors would usually deposit their records with the Exchequer, in case they should be needed for future reference, the Exchequer was playing a purely formal part. In 1478, following the attainder of Edward's brother, the Duke of Clarence, the Warwick, Salisbury and Spencer estates passed to the crown, and these valuable properties, which by the end of the reign were producing £3,500 per year, were dealt with by specially appointed commissioners. These *ad hoc* auditing commissions were under the general control of Edward's Treasurer of the Chamber, Sir Thomas Vaughan, a key figure in the financial administration, and the Yorkist Chamber became the centre of English government finance. The exact division of responsibility between the Exchequer and the Chamber, however, was never clearly established, nor was the practice of appointing commissioners for specific accounts ever given formal organisation.

The need for greater systematisation was apparently felt by Richard III, who established a temporary independent audit department, and who also appointed a single auditor to travel from county to county, checking the accounts of royal agents, thereby avoiding the multiplication of special commissions. Richard continued Edward's practice of putting newly acquired lands under the control of 'foreign' auditors, who had merely to declare their accounts at the Exchequer, and the papers of John Russell, Bishop of Lincoln and a prominent civil servant, suggest that schemes for a general reorganisation of the financial system were under consideration [**doc. 2**]. Richard, who had ruled northern England as his brother's lieutenant, was an experienced administrator, and it seems probable that if he had stayed on the throne a more orderly pattern might have been imposed on the somewhat haphazard arrangements for collecting and auditing the various branches of the royal revenue. But Richard had no time to develop his policies, for in 1485 he was defeated and killed at Bosworth.

Part Two

ANALYSIS

3 Finance

THE NEW KING

There was nothing inevitable about Henry Tudor's victory at Bosworth and his accession to the throne of England. His claim by birth was far from strong [Family tree, pp. 150-51]. Born in January 1457 at Pembroke Castle, he was the posthumous son of Edmund Tudor, who had been created Earl of Richmond by his half-brother Henry VI. Edmund's mother was Catherine of France, who had first been married to Henry V and, after his death, took as her second husband one of her household officers, Owen Tudor, who came from an old Welsh family. Henry's effective claim to the throne came, however, through his mother, Margaret Beaufort, who was directly descended from Edward III through the marriage of his third son, John of Gaunt, Duke of Lancaster, to Catherine Swynford. But Catherine's children had been born before she became the legitimate wife of John of Gaunt, and although an Act of parliament in Richard II's reign removed the stain of illegitimacy from the Beauforts, Henry IV had a clause (of doubtful validity) inserted excluding them from any claim to the throne.

Henry was brought up by his uncle Jasper Tudor, Earl of Pembroke, until 1468, when the boy was captured at Harlech by the Yorkist Lord Herbert. His period of captivity was brief, for in the following year Lord Herbert was taken by the Lancastrians and executed, and in 1470 Henry came once again under the care and guardianship of Jasper Tudor. But the Lancastrian triumph was shortlived. At the battle of Barnet, in May 1471, Henry VI was captured and shortly afterwards murdered, and his only son was killed. Henry Tudor was now the head of the Lancastrian family and fled with his uncle Jasper to Brittany, to wait for better times and to plan a Lancastrian comeback.

For fourteen years Henry was in exile, but throughout that time he kept in touch with the leaders of the Lancastrian cause in

England, and watched for a suitable opportunity to return. Such a moment seemed to come shortly after Richard III had claimed the throne, when his former ally, the Duke of Buckingham, rose in rebellion against him. Henry was deeply involved in Buckingham's rebellion, and the plan was that he should land in England with an army of five thousand men. But the rebellion broke out prematurely, Buckingham was captured and executed, and although Henry set sail his ships were dispersed in a storm, and when he arrived off the English coast near Plymouth he decided not to land.

We know nothing of Henry's feelings at this particular moment, but he would not have been human unless he had felt disappointed and depressed. The life of a pretender, permanently in exile, had little to be said for it, and every failure was followed by the desertion of friends and followers. The Duke of Brittany could not afford to antagonise the apparently powerful king of England, and in September 1484 Henry fled to France to avoid being handed over to Richard's emissaries. He could not risk waiting too long before making another attempt at invasion. Every year that passed strengthened the Yorkist hold on the throne, and Henry feared that Richard was planning to marry Edward IV's daughter, Elizabeth of York (a course of action which Henry himself intended to follow), thereby making even stronger his claim to be the rightful occupant of the English throne. The only hopeful sign, from Henry's point of view, was Richard's unpopularity. Whether or not Richard had actually murdered the princes in the Tower, it was widely assumed that he had done so, and although he was not without redeeming features and was a long way removed from the hunchback villain of Shakespeare's play, Richard was feared rather than loved.

Henry decided to try Wales, his native land, where he could expect to raise supporters, and in August 1485 he sailed from Harfleur. A week later he landed in Milford Haven, not far from his birthplace, and marched rapidly inland. He had borrowed money from France to hire mercenaries, which he brought with him, and as he moved across Wales volunteers came in to join him. But Henry's small army would have been no match for Richard's forces, as long as these remained faithful to the king. Richard was an experienced soldier, unlike Henry who had never fought a battle, and would be assured of victory if only he could rely on the support of the lords he had summoned to fight for him. Richard had issued a general summons to arms, but there was no popular rising in his favour: the indentured retainers who came to fight on his side at Bosworth did so at the command of their lords, and Henry hoped—not without assurance—that when the moment of decision came these lords would hold back, or even switch their allegiance. A key figure in his calculations was Thomas, Lord Stanley, and his brother Sir William Stanley, and Henry had the advantage here in that Lord Stanley had become the third husband of Lady Margaret Beaufort, and was therefore Henry's stepfather.

Henry had his uncle Jasper, an experienced soldier, to advise him, and also the veteran warrior John de Vere, thirteenth Earl of Oxford. But if the outcome of Bosworth had depended on straight fighting, Henry would never have won. In fact the outcome was decided by treachery. Lord Stanley took no part in the battle, but watched to see which way it would go. His brother, Sir William, with three thousand men, held back until the critical moment when Henry was in danger, and then attacked Richard in the rear. Richard knew that the game was up. With a cry of 'Treachery!' he plunged into the heart of the battle and was struck down. The circlet of gold which had adorned his brow fell off and was picked up by Lord Stanley, who placed it on Henry's head. Richard's naked body was slung over a horse and carried ignominiously away to Leicester [**doc. 1**].

The new king of England was a young man of twenty-eight, who was a virtual stranger to his kingdom, having spent most of his early life in Wales and the rest of his time in exile. He was slim, taller than average, and his face, with its straight, Roman nose, its pronounced cheekbones, and its large, rather hooded eyes, was one of considerable nobility. We are accustomed to think of Henry as a silent, grave man, whose countenance, as Bacon said, 'was reverend, and a little like a churchman', but this is only part of the picture [**doc. 32**]. It is true that he aged quickly, and that he cultivated discretion to such a point that men could not be certain what he was thinking. But he also had something of his granddaughter Elizabeth's liveliness of wit; he was very fond of music, buying organs and lutes for his family; and he built a library and encouraged the development of printing in England. 'For his pleasures,' says Bacon, 'there is no news of them', but Henry was far from ascetic. Like English monarchs before and after him he was passionately addicted to hunting and to country life in general, and he took particular

21

delight in exotic animals, establishing a menagerie at the Tower, with lions, leopards, wild cats and rare birds. He enjoyed playing cards and dicing, and had an endearing weakness for clowns and buffoons: visitors to his court encountered, among more majestic figures, 'the foolyshe duc of Lancastre', Dego, the Spanish jester, and Scot and Dick, the master fools.

EXCHEQUER AND CHAMBER

That Henry was fond of money is widely known, but this was more than a miser's senseless addiction. He told Henry Wyatt, one of his councillors and father of the poet, that 'the kings my predecessors, weakening their treasure, have made themselves servants to their subjects', and it was apparent to any intelligent observer that the effectiveness of royal government depended to a large extent upon its wealth. Rich kings were not necessarily strong, but poor ones were bound to be weak.

Henry was not an innovator when it came to financial matters. It is arguable that the monarchy was underendowed and that it needed sources of income more closely related to national wealth instead of depending upon the limited resources of feudal lordship, even though, in this single case, the lordship embraced the whole of England. But whether or not Henry recognised the need for reform, and there is no evidence that he did, he never attempted it. For one thing, he knew that any proposal to raise money from new sources would arouse suspicion and probably encourage the disorder he wished to prevent. And, for another, the Yorkists had shown that the existing revenues of the crown could be expanded in such a way as to make the king solvent and to give him the financial stability he needed. Consciously or unconsciously he followed the policy of Edward IV, of whom one chronicler says 'he turned all his thoughts to the question of how he might in future collect, out of his own substance and by the exercise of his own energy, an amount of treasure worthy of his royal station'.

Henry began, like Edward IV, with a general Act of Resumption, which was passed in 1486 and nominally restored to the crown all the lands which it had held in October 1455. There were, however, many exemptions to this statute, and although a second Act of

Resumption was passed in the following year, Henry really laid claim to little more than Richard III had held. The main object of these Acts was not to give Henry possession of his subjects' property, but to make sure that in the many cases where ownership was disputed and uncertain, the crown would be well placed to assert its own claims. Henry's first parliament assured him the revenues of the duchies of Lancaster and Cornwall, and the earldoms of Richmond and Chester, and constant additions to the royal lands were made throughout the reign by the use of attainder; 138 Acts of attainder were passed against individuals in Henry's reign, and although a third of these were reversed the net effect was a considerable transfer of property to the crown. Attainder was not used primarily as a weapon to strike down the aristocracy; its main impact was felt by smaller men. But some of the confiscations resulting from it were big windfalls for the crown. Sir William Stanley's estate, for instance, brought in £9,000 in cash and £1,000 a year, and the steady addition of attainted estates, as well as the exploitation of established rights, put a considerable strain upon the existing financial machinery.

In the early years of Henry's reign the royal Chamber, which had become under the Yorkists a national treasury, suffered a setback, since Henry was inexperienced in financial affairs and was concerned primarily with keeping the throne he had just gained and defending himself against pretenders. During this period the Exchequer, of necessity, resumed control. But the basic faults of the Exchequer remained. It was not designed for estate administration, and had neither the officials nor the techniques to cope with this. Exploitation demanded something more flexible and more easily able to operate within the interstices of the common law. The Chamber, which could be so closely supervised by the king, and had functions which were capable of indefinite expansion simply because they had never been defined, was the ideal body for this, and as Henry reformed his financial administration he included in it—once again of necessity, since trained administrators were in short supply—many former Yorkist officials, who took up again where Edward IV and Richard III had left off.

The Duchy of Lancaster, which had come to the crown with Henry IV, played a key role in royal finances. Not only was it a valuable part of the royal inheritance, bringing in about £3,500 a year at the close of Edward IV's reign, but it had its own organisation, centred around its chancellor, and was renowned for its efficiency. There was nothing exceptional about the administrative mechanism of the duchy, except perhaps its thoroughness, and many great estates were run on much the same pattern. But since it had never developed semi-autonomous institutions, like the national Exchequer and Chancery, it could operate more effectively and more directly than the royal administration in matters of finance. This was Henry's model, as it had earlier been that of Edward and Richard. Since the English king was also the largest landholder in the country, it was to his advantage to do what other lords did and exploit his estate. The revenues of the Duchy were among the first which Henry withdrew from Exchequer control and gave to specially appointed auditors, and he appointed a trusted servant, Sir Reginald Bray, to be Chancellor of the Duchy and to make sure that its administration operated efficiently.

Bray was one of Henry's few intimate friends and close advisers, and although, as Chancellor of the Duchy, his 'official' sphere of operation was limited, in fact he became chief financial adviser to the king [**doc. 21**]. It was typical of household organisation, and indeed one of its main virtues from Henry's point of view, that a man's influence was proportionate not to the office he held but to the extent to which he was in the personal confidence of the king. As time went on the influence of individuals became formalised into the defined, and therefore limited, responsibilities of departments—the normal development of administration, from expediency to formality—but under Henry VII experiment and informality were the rule. This is what distinguishes 'household' government from 'bureaucratic' government, whether of the medieval or later modern variety. Henry VII's government was less sophisticated than that of, for instance, Edward I, less circumscribed by established institutions and by tradition. This was an indication of Henry's own success in re-establishing royal authority; but it also showed just how weak the crown had become. 'Personal' government was a reaction against impotence and instability, but was essentially an emergency phase. The eventual return to institutional rule, to 'bureaucracy', was a sign of strength.

Before the Chamber could operate effectively it had to be freed from the demands made on it by the royal household; and the expenditure of the household—which, during the late Lancastrian period, had become a bottomless purse through which the revenues of the crown drained away—had to be limited. In 1483, shortly before his death, Edward IV had revived the practice of parliamentary appropriations for the household, whereby certain Exchequer revenues were earmarked for household expenditure and a limit was fixed upon the amount that could be spent. This measure may have been designed as a safeguard in the event of an administrative and financial collapse following Edward's death and the accession of a minor. In fact the control of the administration by Richard, first as protector and then as king, ensured that there was no collapse, and he ignored the Parliamentary appropriation and provided for the household out of his own land revenues. With the accession of a new and inexperienced king in 1485 pressure from the Commons revived and led to a new appropriation, of £14,000 per annum. Ten years later, after complaints by the Commons of the ineffectiveness of this measure, it was replaced by an appropriation of a little over £13,000 a year. Of the two household departments which traditionally dealt with finance, the Wardrobe continued to act as a household treasury, and the Keeper of the Wardrobe remained a court official with no national significance. The Chamber, on the other hand, became once again a national treasury, and its Treasurer was in effect the Treasurer of the kingdom. The actual cash was kept by the Keeper of the Jewels, although the Clerk of the Jewels, nominally his inferior, was in effective control; instructions for its disposal were issued by the king's secretary and his clerks; and officials directly responsible to the Chamber were appointed to operate in the localities.

FEUDAL AND PREROGATIVE REVENUE

Moneys paid in direct to the Chamber came from two main sources. First of all there were the revenues from estates, such as the duchies of Lancaster and Cornwall, which, from about 1487 onwards, were withdrawn from Exchequer control. These revenues were swelled by lands which came to the crown during Henry's reign by course of attainder or escheat. Secondly there were the profits from the exploitation of the crown's prerogative. It was the uncertainty about the nature and extent of the crown's prerogative which made it capable of such remarkable, and lucrative, expansion under a determined king. There were two main aspects to this prerogative.

Analysis

In the first place the king, as the greatest of all feudal lords, had the rights which any lord could claim. He could demand an aid in the specified three cases of ransoming his own body, the marriage of his eldest daughter, and knighting his eldest son—though the consent of his tenants-in-chief (which meant, in fact, of parliament) was necessary before these could be legitimately levied. He could also demand, as a matter of course, the feudal incidents. When a tenant-in-chief (i.e. one who held directly from the crown) died, his land in theory reverted to the king. In practice, however, his heir was allowed to take possession on condition that he paid a sum called relief to the crown. If the heir was under age he became a ward of the king, supposedly to preserve him from harm, and his estates passed under royal guardianship—to compensate the king for the loss of military service which the minority of the heir implied. The king, in fact, would sell the wardship of the minor to the highest bidder, thereby making a welcome capital sum, and he could be sure of a big demand since the man who acquired guardianship of a ward usually acquired the control of his estates until the ward came of age [**doc. 20**]. Despoiling the estate was forbidden by law, but despoiling was an uncertain term, and the high price paid for wardships suggests that those who bought them calculated on making a big profit. Even when the unfortunate minor came of age he or she was not allowed to take over the inheritance until the king had received payment of livery. Wardship did not necessarily involve the intervention of a third party. A mother or other relative could apply for the wardship of the minor, and this might well be granted—but only, of course, upon payment.

Although wardship and livery were the most lucrative of the feudal incidents to which the crown could lay claim, they were not the only ones. If the heir was a woman, the king had the right to control her marriage—in theory, once again, so that her lands should not pass into the possession of his enemies—and this was also a source of profit. The king would either sell the right to marry the heiress, or, if the unfortunate woman was rich enough, would sell her the privilege of deciding her own fate. If there was no heir the king would claim the right of escheat, and take the lands back into his own hands. He could exercise this right also if a tenant-in-chief was found to be a lunatic or an idiot. The theory behind all these incidents dated from the earlier medieval period, when the military organisation of the country really did depend upon the knight-service of tenants-in-chief. By the time Henry came to the throne indentured retainers and commissions of array (p. 47) had replaced feudal obligations as an effective source of raising armies, but feudalism, deprived of its original *raison d'être*, remained in existence as a financial system.

In addition to his feudal prerogative, the king had rights which belonged to him as king. Some of these—such as the right to issue proclamations and to pardon—were long-established and reasonably well defined, and much of what had at one time been the king's prerogative had come to be exercised through the courts of common law. In theory the kingship of England was limited. The king acknowledged his obligations in his coronation oath, and the cooperation between the monarch and his subjects—which Fortescue claimed as typical of the English limited monarchy, in contrast to the absolutism of the French—was expressed in the fact that the king could make no new law nor raise new taxation without the consent of his subjects in parliament. Yet although the fifteenth-century insistence on limitation was not without foundation as far as the realities of the situation were concerned, there was another side to the picture. Fifteenth-century thought in Europe as a whole put great emphasis upon the authority of the king, as a counter-weight to disorder, and Bishop Russell, in 1483, said that the ruler was, as it were, a god in the land. As the guardian of his subjects, the king of England had a duty, as well as a right, to make them live in peace and good order, to punish those who resisted, to take bonds of good behaviour, and to supplement the course of the common law where this was deficient. After the breakdown of effective government in the second half of the fifteenth century, such an initiative was generally welcomed by property-owners, but by the end of Henry VII's reign they were only too aware of the danger to themselves that such an ill-defined prerogative created. In his 'royal', as in his 'feudal' prerogative, lack of definition left the way open for negotiation, and in all such matters the king drove a hard bargain.

Feudal incidents, and particularly wardship, were resented by the landowners, who frequently sought to evade them. In a country where communications were poor, the existence of an under-age heir, or of an heiress, could be concealed, with the connivance of neighbours and a possible bribe to local officials. Where conceal-ment was not practised, the tenant could take refuge in the disorders of the preceding half century and claim that his land was not in fact held 'in chief' and was not therefore liable to feudal incidents. Henry's reply to such methods of evasion was to appoint commissions, from early in his reign, to enquire into his prerogative rights, and for this purpose he revived the medieval institution of the sworn inquest. Laboriously but inexorably the commissioners pursued their enquiries, ferreted out concealed heirs, and replied to claims of uncertain tenure by asserting that in all doubtful cases the land should be regarded as belonging to the crown. The commissioners for concealments who were at work in 1504-9, for instance, discovered that Lord Powys, who had died ten years earlier, had held lands in chief, but that for most of this time Lord Dudley had taken the profits 'but how, or by what title, the jurors knew not'. Another commission 'post-mortem', enquiring into the estates of landowners after their death, uncovered a minor heir, aged two; and the last fifty inquisitions post-mortem calendared for the reign reveal twenty-eight under-age heirs. The average life span in Henry VII's England was short by modern standards; hence the frequency of inheritance by minors, and the significance of wardship. Landowners could, however, appeal to the common law courts against unfavourable decisions by royal commissioners, and might well succeed. In 1505, for instance, a royal commission in Northumberland ruled that twenty tenancies of the Earl of Northumberland belonged of right to the crown. King's Bench, however, on an appeal by the tenants, reversed most of these verdicts.

THE PROBLEM OF COORDINATION

As the number of commissions enquiring into the crown's rights increased, the problem of coordinating their activities made itself apparent. The extent of the various enquiries is shown in Professor Richardson's summary of the items of revenue, which came from
concealed lands, wards, marriages, reliefs, escheats, goods of outlaws, felons and fugitives, natural fools, forfeiture and concealment of offices, land given in mortmain or alienated without licence, and intrusion upon lands held in chief of the crown . . . extortions, falsifications, contempts, concealed escheats, usuries, treasure trove, goods of fugitives, felons and outlaws, destruction and sale of woods, widows whose marriages belonged to the king,

rape of heirs who remained under the jurisdiction of the crown, enclosures without licence, intrusions without due livery after the death of ancestors, unpaid loans or special debts due the king, lands and mines leased for a specified term of years, offences against the statutes of liveries, embezzlement of crown property, advowsons of churches claimed by the crown, offences against the customs, murder, riots, and unlawful assemblies (**32**, pp. 120-21).

General supervision of all this activity was carried out by Bray and the Treasurer of the Chamber. This last office was held by Thomas Lovell from the beginning of Henry's reign until 1492, when he became Treasurer of the Household and was replaced at the Chamber by his second-in-command John Heron. Bray, Lovell, Heron, and another official, Sir Robert Southwell, were in effect a body of auditors, but the practice of auditing preceded the establishment of any formal court of audit, and Henry's own involvement in the day-to-day financial administration held back what would now seem to be the normal development from *ad hoc* appointments to the establishment of departments. Henry checked the Treasurer of the Chamber's accounts, initialling the pages as he did so, and at the end of every year he was given a 'declaration' of the state of the Chamber treasury. This was paralleled by an annual declaration from the Exchequer—which, after 1505, simply accepted the reports of the king's specially appointed auditors, and confined its own elaborate system of audit to the decreasing number of revenue items still under its control. After Bray's death in 1503, Heron, although he still submitted his accounts to the king, was given a fairly free hand, and it is possible that if Henry had lived longer he would have relaxed his tight control sufficiently to enable an auditing office—something perhaps on the lines of the later Court of General Surveyors—clearly to emerge. But as it was, the officials were more important than their offices, and organisation remained embryonic.

One branch of the financial administration was, however, given a more clearly defined shape. This was wardship, which became of greater and greater importance as the reign progressed. In 1487 the income from wardship was under £350, but by 1494 it was over £1,500 and by 1507 it had rocketed to more than £6,000. At first Henry appointed household officials *ad hoc* to deal with wardship, but as the revenue increased the need for specialisation became apparent. This was especially the case after the death of Bray, and in 1503, therefore, Sir John Hussey was appointed to the new office of Master of Wards, with the responsibility for 'overseeing, managing and selling the wardships of all lands which may be in the king's hands'. As Hussey built up a staff and an organisation, the king ceased to take such an active interest in wardship, and Hussey, Master of Wards in fact as well as name, extended his grip until it covered the whole country. It seems probable that by 1509 there were local masters of wards, receiver-generals and auditors for every county, all responsible to Hussey, who was, of course, responsible to the king.

The lack of centralisation was a weakness in Henry's system, and although the king, by acting as his own chief auditor, filled the gap, it made a heavy strain upon him, especially as he had many other matters to deal with. In the early years of his reign it was understandable that he should trust no man and insist on being his own inspector-general, but as he grew older and more firmly established on the throne he built up a corps of officials —men like Bray, Lovell, Heron and Southwell—who were trustworthy and devoted to his service. In 1508, therefore, the office of Surveyor of the King's Prerogative was created, and was entrusted to Sir Edward Belknap. The authority of the Surveyor did not extend to all the prerogative rights of the crown—wardship for instance, was excluded—but was designed to deal mainly, though not exclusively, with revenues arising from the king's 'royal', rather than his 'feudal', prerogative. Belknap was required to take over the property of persons who had been attainted, outlawed, or convicted of any offence that entailed confiscation of possessions, and to make the necessary arrangements for leasing or selling it. He had his agents in the localities, like the Master of Wards, and could call on sheriffs and justices of the peace for assistance. His work brought him into close association with Empson and Dudley, who used the process of outlawry to recover fines imposed by the king's Council or the common law courts (see p. 35). It was this association with men who came to be identified with the more extortionate aspects of Henry's rule that led to the winding-up of the office of Surveyor of the Prerogative early in Henry VIII's reign. Belknap himself survived, but the delimitation of responsibilities which his appointment had foreshadowed died with his office. Not until the emergence of Thomas Cromwell in the 1530s did the rationalisation of the financial administration gather momentum.

HENRY'S ACHIEVEMENT

The simplest way of demonstrating Henry's achievement in restoring the royal finances would be to compare his annual revenue with that of his immediate predecessors, but this is far from easy. Tudor accounting systems were not designed to produce this type of clearcut picture, and it is doubtful if even Henry VII himself knew how much money to expect every year. The most reliable estimates (**64**) seem to be that during the period 1485–1509 the income from royal lands went up by forty-five per cent, from £29,000 to £42,000, while the customs revenue increased by just over twenty per cent, from £33,000 to £40,000. By the end of the reign the Chamber was handling a little over £91,000 a year, on the average, while the Exchequer received about £12,500. If a further £10,000 is added for other sources of income, this gives a total revenue of something over £113,000 a year.

These figures do not, of course, tell the whole story. Certain revenues—varying in amount from the thousands of pounds paid annually to the Treasurer of Calais by the Company of the Staple to the small sums which sheriffs and other royal officials were allowed to deduct from their receipts for their salaries and expenses—never passed through the central receiving agencies. Even more difficult to assess is the 'concealed income' from such things as grants or sales of wardships and offices: when the king rewarded one of his servants by granting him a lucrative office, or by selling him a wardship at a nominal sum, he was saving himself money, and this is, in effect, a form of income. But even when generous allowance has been made for all these indirect sources of profit to the crown, it is unlikely that the royal revenue would come anywhere near the £1,100,000 enjoyed by the Emperor, or even the £800,000 which the King of France could expect every year. Henry VII had the reputation of being a rich king, but this was only because he lived well within his income. He could not afford the extravagances of his fellow monarchs, especially the extravagance of war. When Henry VIII attempted to pursue more grandiloquent policies which he thought appropriate to his royal dignity, he swiftly exhausted his inheritance. Recognition of Henry VII's achievement in restoring the royal finances must not obscure the fact that by continental standards the English crown was underendowed, circumscribed in its freedom of action, and dependent upon the acquiescence, if not the goodwill, of those who were subject to it.

4 Administration

THE COUNCIL

Henry VII's Council, in its composition and range of activities, was virtually the same as that of Edward IV and Richard III, and twenty of Richard's councillors served Henry in the same capacity. The largest group within the Council consisted of clerics, and one of Henry's most trusted advisers was John Morton, appointed Chancellor in 1487 and later made a cardinal and Archbishop of Canterbury. Richard Fox, the king's secretary and later Keeper of the Privy Seal, who became Bishop of Winchester, was another important figure; so was William Warham, who took Morton's place as Chancellor and eventually became Archbishop of Canterbury.

The nobles were also represented, and there was no sign under Henry VII any more than there had been under Edward IV of a deliberate attempt to oust them from government. Ability and loyalty were the only requirements so far as Henry was concerned, and prominent among the nobles on the Council was John de Vere, thirteenth Earl of Oxford, who had fought with Henry at Bosworth and was rewarded with the offices of Great Chamberlain and Lord Admiral. Henry did not confine membership of the Council to those who had fought for him. Thomas Howard, Earl of Surrey, who had been among Richard's adherents at Bosworth and had suffered for his loyalty to the crown by being imprisoned in the Tower, was released after three years and appointed to the Council; and during the early years of the reign the Earl of Lincoln, one of the Yorkist leaders and the inspiration behind Lambert Simnel's rebellion, was a regular attender.

But although Henry's Council contained representatives of the nobility, few of them were really to be numbered among the king's intimate advisers, and to this extent the traditional picture of Henry as a man who distrusted the nobility is true. There was no parallel to the sort of influence that the magnates had wielded in the Minority Council of Henry VI, for the king himself took all the decisions, and accepted or rejected advice as he saw fit. His chief secular advisers and servants were drawn not from the aristocracy but from the lesser landowners and professional men, especially lawyers. These were 'middle class' only to the extent that they were lower in degree than the nobles and higher than the masses, but the term is too misleading to be of value. In their assumptions and aspirations—and often in their family connections —these men were very close to the landed aristocracy, and were in fact part of the upper, or governing, section of English society. They were 'new' only to the extent that their ancestors had not been numbered among the principal servants of the crown in earlier centuries; but in local government they had generations of experience behind them. Lovell, for instance, came from a long line of country gentlemen, and had been trained as a lawyer. Dudley was the grandson of a Lancastrian peer. Belknap's family traced its descent from one of the Conqueror's companions, and he counted a chief justice among his ancestors. Poynings was the son of a Kentish squire (who had been carver and sword-bearer to Jack Cade at the time of Cade's rebellion!), and his mother was a Paston. Empson, whose father was one of the leading citizens of Towcester, seems to have been the only 'new man' on Henry's Council who came from a bourgeois background. The rest were nearly all from gentry families, and had made their way in the world either through the law or through estate management. So much of Henry's wealth derived from the exploitation of his lands that he needed men who were skilled in estate management and conversant with the intricate law of property. These qualifications, rather than social position, were the characteristics of his lay councillors.

Although the names of some two hundred councillors survive for Henry's reign, these never met all together at any one time. The Council was as large or as small as Henry needed for his immediate purposes, but the average attendance seems to have grown larger as the reign progressed, and meetings of forty or so councillors were by no means uncommon. These were not merely formal assemblies, since the king himself was usually present and important matters were discussed. There are records of smaller meetings at which he was not present, and it seems that, in this reign at any rate, a large Council was a sign of strength rather than weakness.

A Council of forty or so members was likely to be unwieldy, and much of the actual work was delegated to committees of the Council. Edward IV had appointed committees of the Council to deal with the augmentation of his land revenues, and the Tudor Court of Requests had a forerunner in the Council committee set up by Richard III to deal with poor men's causes. Among the Council committees set up in Henry VII's reign was that given statutory authority in 1487 to deal with liveries and maintenance. The statute was later given the erroneous title *Pro Camera Stellata* [**doc. 11**], and was held to be the origin of the Court of Star Chamber: in fact the committee set up by it functioned separately from the whole Council sitting in Star Chamber—though there was, of course, an overlap in personnel—and was merely one of several committees appointed to deal with specific problems or groups of problems. The surveyors of land revenues, whose existence can be traced after 1493, was another.

THE COUNCIL LEARNED

The most notorious of all such Council committees was the 'Council Learned in the Law'. This was a small committee, and the king was never present at its deliberations. It had close connections with the Duchy of Lancaster, since the Chancellor of the Duchy seems to have acted as a kind of president, and the clerk of the council of the Duchy acted as its clerk. It usually met in the Duchy chamber, but some meetings apparently took place in houses belonging to one or other of the members. The Council Learned was in existence from at least 1500, and Bray, as Chancellor of the Duchy, played a prominent part in its proceedings. But its reputation—or rather its ill fame—increased after Sir Richard Empson became Chancellor of the Duchy in 1504. Empson was a lawyer, trained in land administration, and his close associate was Edmund Dudley, a former under-sheriff of London, who became Speaker in 1504. Empson and Dudley had been friends and colleagues of Bray, and had presumably learnt many of their methods under him.

The Council Learned dealt with a great variety of cases—for instance the exportation of wool without paying customs dues; the transference of land to a corporation without licence of mortmain; failure to take up knighthood; misconduct of sheriffs; and infringement of the king's prerogative of wardship and livery. It also acted as a debt-collecting agency for the Chamber, and much of the work of Empson and Dudley consisted in compounding with offenders and with debtors for moneys which were owed the crown. Some of the amounts involved were very large—like the £10,000 demanded from the Earl of Northumberland in 1506 for ravishing one of the king's wards—but they were rarely collected in full. The king used them as a sort of probation system by leaving the remitted part of the fine to be collected only in case of further misconduct.

The complaints made against the Council Learned were that it operated without a jury, and that too much discretion was left to its members where the fixing of penalties was involved. There was nothing exceptional about operating without a jury, of course: this was true of conciliar activity as a whole, and was increasingly practised because the effectiveness of the jury system had been eroded by bastard feudalism. As for the lack of certainty about the sums demanded, this varied with the nature of the case. Many of the largest fines were imposed by common law courts. Where offences concerned penal statutes (see p. 62), the fine was sometimes fixed by the statute; but in offences against the king's prerogative, the amount to be paid was a matter for negotiation. This was also the case in that part of the Council's business which was concerned not with offenders but with those who wanted a favour from the king, which might range from hiring his ships to persuading him not to enforce his rights in the case of wardship or lunacy [**doc. 28**].

There is little doubt that Empson and Dudley were ruthless in their enforcement of royal rights, and occasionally guilty of corrupt practices—as in the case of Thomas Sunnyff. Sunnyff was accused by one of Dudley's servants of murdering his (stillborn) child, and Dudley demanded payment of £500, saying 'Agree with the king, or else you must go to the Tower'. When Sunnyff refused, he was imprisoned, and the judges of King's Bench rejected his application for bail on the grounds that they could not disregard the king's commands. Sunnyff eventually paid up, for fear that he would otherwise be left in prison until he died. Dudley later expressed remorse for his action, but insisted that he made not a penny out of it: all the money went to the king. According to Polydore Vergil, the king, who was unwilling to be thought unjust in his actions, 'took thought how he might act with a show of right. As he thought upon this it occurred to him that his people were in the habit of paying so little heed to the laws of the kingdom that if the question were raised, without doubt very many ... would be found guilty of violating them.' That this statement was no mere rhetoric is suggested by Dudley's own reference to a book called *Jura Regalia*, in which the king kept a list of all his legal powers and privileges. It may have contained, among other things, the old statutes which, according to an act of the first year of Henry VIII's reign, had not been 'put in execution till now of late' [**doc. 33**].

It is undoubtedly true that the activities of Empson and Dudley aroused the anger of the propertied classes, and led to their execution after Henry VII's death. But although they may have been more efficient, and possibly less scrupulous, than Bray, their work was essentially the same. The thoroughness of the king's commissions of enquiry is shown by the fact that even the chief men in the kingdom could not escape them. When the commissioners at work in Hampshire in 1508 found that some of the manors which Dudley had inherited belonged, in fact, to the crown, Dudley had to sue for pardon from the king for intruding on these estates (albeit unintentionally) without paying livery. No wonder lesser men complained of the king's severity! Henry framed the policy which the commissioners executed, and this policy had not changed since the beginning of the reign [**doc. 29**]. It consisted in the enforcement of the king's rights, and the collection of moneys to which he had any claim—however slender.

Such a policy was bound to be resented by those who had taken advantage of years of disorder to abandon their obligations. In the early years of the reign they were prepared to accept this as the price to be paid for a return to normality; but by the sixteenth century, when the recollection of the Wars of the Roses was fading and relative order and stability were coming to be taken for granted, it may well have seemed intolerable [**doc. 31**]. Historians have disputed over the justice of Henry's policy, but in such matters 'justice' is a relative term. The real question is 'What is a reasonable price to pay for the benefit of good order and government?', and the answer to this will vary from individual to individual, and from generation to generation.

One thing, at any rate, seems clear: that although Empson, Dudley, and other royal servants, profited from their service to the crown, Henry was by far the biggest beneficiary. Dudley's account book survives, and shows that in 1506–07 he collected £60,000 in money and recognizances for the king. Even if there were other amounts, unrecorded, which he kept for himself, they cannot possibly have come to more than a small fraction of this enormous sum. In any case, most of this total was in the form of promises to pay, and only about a quarter was in hard cash. The debts were duly listed in the king's books, for possible future collection. As a system of law enforcement this was crude, and Henry VIII, shortly after his accession, cancelled all outstanding debts to the crown. But Henry VIII had the advantage of coming to a throne that was comparatively secure and to a country that was relatively ordered. The hard, and often dirty, work of accomplishing this had been done by his father.

THE COMMON LAW

In its combination of administrative and judicial action the Council Learned was a microcosm of the Council as a whole. The king had a duty, as well as a right, to provide justice for his subjects, and although this duty, earlier in the middle ages, had been given formal embodiment in the common law, with its courts and judges, the king's capacity for justice was not thereby exhausted: in theory, at any rate, the fountain of justice never ran dry. Had the common law been a flexible instrument and kept itself up-to-date, there would have been little need for further intervention by the crown. But almost from its inception the royal initiative in law had been challenged by the barons, and they secured that no new forms of writ should be developed after Edward I's reign. This meant that the forms of law were suddenly rigidified at a time when society was changing rapidly. The lawyers might have kept up pressure for reform, but instead they made a virtue of necessity, accepting the limitations that had been imposed upon them, and creating complicated devices whereby the law could be made to apply to cases in which it had no obvious competence. The result was no doubt satisfying to the legal mind, and was in many ways a masterpiece of ingenuity. But to the outsider the law was a complicated jungle, and the gap between what was morally and what was legally right became wider and wider.

The machinery of the law was as inadequate as its actual provisions. The courts at Westminster were in session for the four

37

legal terms only, and since each of these occupied no more than three weeks it meant that justice could be done for a mere three months in the year. This limited provision was further restricted by the fact that the judges sat for only three hours each day, and that proceedings were conducted in Norman-French—a dialect which, by Henry VII's time if not before, was incomprehensible to anybody outside the legal profession.

The ineffectiveness of the courts was matched by the ineffectiveness of the procedure for bringing criminals to book. There was no police force, and the village constable was more often than not a figure of fun. Even when offenders were pursued, by the sheriff or other interested parties, they could claim sanctuary in parish churches, churchyards, and innumerable other places. In the unlikely event of their being actually arrested they still had a good chance of escaping conviction. Those who could read could claim benefit of clergy; others could escape justice on the grounds that the indictment against them contained an error, no matter how trivial, since complete verbal accuracy was obligatory. If all these expedients failed, there was always the jury to rely upon. Lawyers professed a high regard for the jury system, but in fact juries were as corruptible and as subject to influence as any private individual [**doc. 18**]. The inadequacy of the jury system had been exposed during the period of Henry VI's minority and the Wars of the Roses, when there had been plenty of law but little order and little justice.

THE COUNCIL IN STAR CHAMBER

It was to counter the rigidification of the common law that the equitable jurisdiction of the king-in-Council had developed in the fourteenth and early fifteenth centuries, but by the time Henry VII came to the throne nearly all the cases involving equity had come to be dealt with by the Chancellor—the keeper of the king's conscience—and the Court of Chancery had moved out of the household much as the Exchequer and the King's Bench had done several centuries earlier. The creation of a court of equity did not, however, solve all the problems which resulted from the conservatism of the common law in face of prevailing disorder. What was needed was some body powerful enough not to be over-ridden by even the greatest men in the realm, and able to act as a clearing-house for difficult cases, passing them on to the appropriate court. This was the judicial function of the Council in Henry VII's reign and it kept an ever-watchful eye upon the administration of law, taking action to remedy weaknesses and to redress injustice.

The Council sat to do justice in one or other of the two rooms that made up the Star Chamber. Proceedings could be initiated by a petition to the king, in which verbal slips made no difference; there was no jury; the defendant was examined on oath; and decisions were reached on grounds of common sense rather than law—although the presence on the Council of the two chief justices, and the legal training of many of the other Councillors, meant that the prevailing assumptions were those of the common law. There were limitations upon the Council's activity as a judicial body. A statute of Edward III's reign had forbidden it to deal with cases concerning freehold or franchise, and although this limitation was not strictly observed it had come to be interpreted as meaning that the Council could not inflict the death penalty nor order mutilation (though this latter limitation did not prevent it, on occasion, from ordering the loss of ears). This placed the Council at a disadvantage in dealing with serious cases, in which the loss of life or limb was likely to be involved, and was presumably one of the reasons for the appointment of the conciliar committee in 1487 (see p. 34), given authority by statute to punish such cases 'after the form and effect of statutes thereof made, in like manner and form as they should and ought to be punished if [the offenders] were thereof convict after the due order of the law'.

Had the Council in Star Chamber acted primarily as a court of appeal, dealing with particularly difficult matters, the limitations upon its freedom of action would have been a severe handicap. But in many instances, perhaps the majority, it did not initiate action itself. The records of just under two hundred cases dealt with by the Council in Star Chamber survive for Henry VII's reign, and most of these are concerned with disputes between party and party in which the crown was not directly involved. Livery and maintenance rarely appear, and there is not a single instance of retaining. This suggests that the principal work of the Council consisted in making the common law courts act more efficiently, and many cases were in fact referred to the King's Bench or other courts with instructions on how they should be dealt with. The Council registers, however, show that the surviving records of actual cases do not tell the whole story. The Council did initiate actions, and was particularly concerned with offences against public order, even though the detailed records of these cases do not survive. It punished retaining and rioting, summoned breakers of the peace before it, examined corrupt juries, and took cognizance of unlawful assemblies, perjury, maintenance and contempt of court. These were, after all, the prevailing offences of the day, and it seems unlikely, even without the corroboration of the registers, that the Council would have taken no action against them.

The Council in Star Chamber had a civil jurisdiction as well as a criminal one, and dealt, among other things, with municipal and trade disputes, such as that between the Staplers and the Merchant Adventurers (see pp. 68-69). Much of its time, however—indeed perhaps most of its time—was spent in settling disputes between individuals which were brought to its attention by petition from one or other of the parties concerned, and it was demand from below rather than imposition from above which caused the expansion of the Council's judicial activity. Such disputes could usually have been settled by the normal processes of the common law, but plaintiffs often preferred to petition the Council. If the Council passed their case on to a common law court to be dealt with, they would at least be sure of speedier action than if the law was left to take its usual course; and if the Council dealt with the matter itself, the judgment was final and there could be no appeal. Certainty and swiftness were often preferable to judicial niceties [**doc. 17**].

The Council in Star Chamber did not always go through the process of formal trial. Where a case seemed to be clear, or to require swift action, the Council would sometimes issue an executive order which assumed the guilt of the accused person—in 1488, for instance, it ordered the Mayor of York to put two men who had spoken against 'our majesty royal' in the pillory, and to cut their ears off. This type of action was usually taken in cases which directly affected the king, since the Council had a particular interest in anything that threatened, or seemed to threaten, the safety of the king and the future of his dynasty. Treason or suspected treason was of immediate concern to them; so were riots, which broke the king's peace and could easily develop into rebellion.

The older picture of the Council in Star Chamber as a powerful body acting with ruthless determination in bringing overmighty offenders to book and in imposing the king's will by administrative action, is only one side of the picture where Henry VII's reign is concerned. Far from being a rival to the courts of common law, it acted as a spur to them and goaded them into action. Certain cases it had to deal with itself. Where the king's interests were directly involved, for instance, the common law judges would not take action without consulting the Council; where parliamentary petitions were left over after the session of parliament had ended, the Council had to decide what action to take; and in those cases where the common law offered either no remedy or an insufficient one, the Council once again had no alternative but to intervene. Generally speaking, however, it supplemented the common law instead of rivalling it, and the jealousy and hostility of the common lawyers which developed later in the century was not apparent in Henry VII's reign.

The Council could be ruthless, where ruthlessness seemed necessary—as is shown by the case quoted above. But its punishments were usually distinguished by moderation rather than severity, and 'Star Chamber justice' had, as far as the surviving records show, none of the harshness associated with it under Laud. Whipping and mutilation were exceptional, and heavy fines were rarely inflicted and even more rarely collected in full. In the words of the historian of the Council in Star Chamber under Henry VII: 'it was surely the mildest-mannered tribunal that ever sentenced a criminal, considerate in its procedure, gentle in its punishments, and failing altogether to live up to the reputation of ruthlessness that the Star Chamber has enjoyed since the seventeenth century (**2,** p. clxxii).

OTHER COUNCILS

The need for justice and order led to the creation of a number of other councils in the late Yorkist–early Tudor period. One of these, the Court of Requests, has already been mentioned. This was a committee of the Council, and was deputed to deal with cases affecting poor men, who could not afford the time and money that an action in the common law courts entailed, and who were obviously susceptible to pressure from those richer than themselves. Edward IV's Council paid particular attention to the affairs of poor men, as is suggested by the appointment of John Harington as a second clerk of the Council in 1483 'for his good service before the lords and others of the Council, especially in the custody, registration, and expedition of bills, requests and supplications of poor persons'. It was left to Richard III to set up a regular tribunal for poor men's causes, but this Court of Requests lapsed in 1485—probably because of the hostility of Parliament, although a Bill to abolish it did not become law. After the conclusion of peace with France in 1493, Henry revived the practice of appointing Councillors to deal specifically with poor men's causes, and by the end of his reign it seems that some degree of specialisation was already beginning to take place. This foreshadowed the later development of the Court of Requests, which became, in its organisation and personnel, quite distinct from the Council itself.

The Council of the North was another body which could trace its origin to the Yorkist period. The north of England was a week's journey from London, and the border area with Scotland was lawless and undisciplined. Forays on either side of the border kept up a state of perpetual warfare, and local inhabitants looked to the great families of the north—the Percies, Nevilles, Cliffords and Dacres—rather than to the king, for protection and for orders. The actual border area was divided into three marches, each under control of a warden, usually a member of one of the leading families, who was responsible for its defence. The east and middle marches were effectively under the control of the Percies, Earls of Northumberland, but their influence was challenged by Richard, Duke of Gloucester, who inherited most of the Neville lands and became one of the most powerful figures in the north. Edward IV trusted his brother more than the magnates, appointed him to a number of offices, large and small, in the royal gift, thereby increasing his prestige, and in 1482 made him lieutenant of the north. Richard had a household council which became the centre for the administration of this area, except for the eastern part where Northumberland and his council maintained order.

Richard's rule in the north was popular, and when he became king he appointed his nephew, the Earl of Lincoln, to govern Yorkshire, and equipped him with a council which had 'authority and power to order and direct all riots, forcible entries . . . and other misbehaviours against our laws and peace committed and done in the said parts; and if such be that they in no wise can thoroughly order, then to refer it unto us and thereof certify us in all goodly haste thereafter'. This was the model on which the later Council of the North was to be based.

Richard left control of the east and middle marches, and in effect of the whole border area, in the hands of the 4th Earl of Northumberland. This arrangement did not suit Henry VII, who disliked the Percies both for their Yorkist sympathies and for their princely power. He appointed the earl as his lieutenant in the north, but he dismissed him from the important captaincy of Berwick, which he transferred to a courtier, and he looked for some opportunity to replace Percy influence by royal influence in the border region. Henry's difficulties in dealing with the magnates are nowhere more apparent than in the north. Commissions of enquiry were at work, there as elsewhere, investigating royal rights, and offenders were summoned to appear before the Council in London. But the vast estates of the Percies gave them a range of patronage and therefore of influence which the crown could not hope to match. What Henry needed was a stroke of good fortune which would give him a foothold in the north, and this came in 1489 when the fourth earl was killed in a riot at Thirsk while acting as a royal tax-collector. The earl's heir was a minor and became a ward of the king. Henry took over the guardianship of his estates and stepped into the Percies' place as effective ruler of the marches. The circumstances surrounding the assassination of the 4th earl were mysterious, and Henry, who stood to gain so much, may well have known more than he chose to reveal (**26**). He could be unscrupulous if it served his purposes, and throughout his reign he used every means—ranging from the careful distribution of patronage to the incitement of family feuds—to build up a royal 'connection' in the north. Northumberland's place as the king's lieutenant in the north was taken by Thomas Howard, Earl of Surrey, but his rule was confined, in effect, to Yorkshire. Henry then made his son, Prince Arthur, nominal Warden-General of the Marches, with Surrey as his underwarden. Royal officials, trained in Chamber organisation, were appointed both to the prince's council and to that which Surrey had as king's lieutenant. Most important of the officials on Surrey's council was William Sever, then an abbot and later Bishop of Carlisle, who was an expert in financial administration and kept in close touch with Bray in London. Sever's duties were to enforce prerogative rights in the north, and his powers—which were the usual mixture of administrative and judicial—were similar to those formally conferred in Henry VIII's reign on the President of the Council of the North. Under Henry VII, however, although much may be inferred, little was explicit, and there is no clear evidence of the existence of a Council of the North during this time. In this respect Henry's reign was a period of retrogression compared with that of the Yorkists.

The marches of Wales were another disturbed area, partly because of the nature of the country and its people, and partly because of its distance from London in an age of poor communications. Edward IV, who, as Earl of March, had been given certain revenues from the Principality of Wales, appointed a council to administer his lands in the marches (the border area between England and Wales), and Henry VII revived this body, appointed his son, Arthur, Prince of Wales, as nominal president, and extended its competence to Wales as well as the royal estates in the marches. This council was not in any sense a committee of the Council which sat in Westminister. Local councils were simply delegations of the king's authority in the areas over which they had control, and they could exercise jurisdiction which was, in certain ways, more extensive even than that of the Council itself.

JUSTICES OF THE PEACE

The authority of prerogative councils was confined to the border areas, where disorder was endemic. For the country as a whole the king depended for the enforcement of his will upon the justices of the peace, who had gradually taken over most of the effective powers of the sheriff, and reduced that office to impotence and unpopularity. The justices of the peace were appointed annually from among the local gentry, and were charged by the commission of the peace with the maintenance of order. Their duties were also increased during the Tudor period by statute, and Henry VII's reign saw an Act of 1487 giving them authority to take bail, and another of 1495 making it lawful for them to act upon information they received, without waiting for formal indictment by a grand jury. Much of the justices' work in any shire was done by a handful of them sitting together as the needs of their situation and their own convenience dictated. But four times a year formal Quarter Sessions were held at which all the justices, and most of the people of importance in the shire, were expected to be present. At these Quarter Sessions the justices tried anyone who had been indicted of any crime except treason—which required a speedy and more powerful investigation—and either dealt with offenders themselves, or, in difficult cases, referred them to the justices of assize.

The justices of the peace were not simply judicial officers. They were also deeply concerned with local administration, and at Quarter Sessions they enquired into the conduct of all local officials, including mayors and sheriffs. The control of agriculture and industry, which had previously been the concern of the feudal (usually manorial) courts, or of the old popular courts of the shire and hundred, was also being taken over by the justices of the peace, and parliament was already beginning to increase their powers in this field. An Act of 1495, for instance, required them to suppress unlawful games and regulate ale-houses, while in 1504 another statute made them responsible for seeing that pewter and brass were of the required fineness. The importance of the justice of the peace can hardly be overestimated. Orders made by the king and his Council were of little use if they could not be enforced, and although the actual machinery which transmitted the royal will to the localities is not always easy to define, or seems to be inadequate for the purpose—like a telephone wire that has gone dead—the justices were at the receiving end.

Henry could rely upon the justices' own natural interest as property owners in the maintenance of peace and good order, and he could always use the threat of removal from the commission of the peace—a blow to a landowner's pride and social standing in an age which valued such things highly. Justices of the peace could be summoned before Chancery or the common law courts to answer charges of maladministration, and King's Bench could override decision of Quarter Sessions when it thought that the justices had failed in their duty. Where there was a general breakdown of order, Henry could also attempt to mobilise public opinion to goad the justices, as is shown by an Act of 1489 in which it was declared that 'by the negligence and misdemeaning, favour, and other inordinate causes of the justice of the peace in every shire of this his realm, the laws and ordinances made for the politic weal, peace and good rule of the same, and for perfect surety and restful living of his subjects of the same, be not duly executed'. The problem was simple—*Quis custodiet ipsos custodies?*—but there was no simple answer. The justices of the peace were ordered to read out a proclamation at Quarter Sessions in which their duties were clearly outlined and which also commanded any man, rich or poor, who had suffered from the negligence or partiality of any justice of the peace, to make his complaint either to the justices of assize or direct to the king. Such primitive and clumsy machinery is hardly likely to have been very effective, and should be regarded more as an expression of intent than an actual remedy.

Paid royal officials, dependent for their living upon the king's pleasure, would have been far more effective from Henry's point of view, and the Spanish ambassador reported that Henry told him 'he would like to govern England in the French fashion, but he cannot'. The reason for Henry's abandonment of his wishes in this respect is not far to seek. A corps of royal officials would have cost more money than the crown had available, and the restoration of royal solvency was one of Henry's main aims. In any case he had inherited from the Middle Ages a system of local administration which, whatever its weaknesses, worked quite well and could no doubt be made to work better, and which cost the crown virtually nothing. Government on the cheap, at the centre as well as in the localities, was one of the characteristics of Tudor England: but it meant, as Kenneth Pickthorn pithily put it, that 'the English government remained very feebly armed before a population which it had not disarmed' (**31**, p. 73).

If the king was dependent upon the justices of the peace, the justices themselves were dependent upon the smaller officials charged with bringing offenders to book. Every hundred was bound by law to provide itself with a high constable, and every parish with a petty constable, and these appointments were usually made by the justices. Such offices were very unpopular, since the remuneration was insignificant and the risks were considerable. The constables were spare-time officials, who could rely only on themselves. There were few volunteers for such posts, and the justices frequently had to use their powers of compulsion to fill them. The consequence was that at this lowest level of society, where the forces of law and order came into closest and most direct contact with the forces of disorder, there was a lack of will and of means. The concern of the justices of the peace in putting down and punishing crime must not blind us to the fact that a great deal of crime went unpunished. The concept of 'order' in Tudor England was relative. By modern standards,

English society before the nineteenth century was a paradise for the criminal.

In cases of riot or rebellion the king could call out his armed forces, but here again shortage of money, as well as the prevailing antipathy towards the idea of a standing army, left the sovereign dependent upon the goodwill of his greater subjects. Henry had a small bodyguard, amounting to something over a hundred men [**doc. 4**], and a few mercenaries in his pay. He also had, at Calais, a garrison of some eight hundred men, which was considered enormous and cost about £10,000 a year to maintain. The Company of the Staple, which was financially responsible for the maintenance of the garrison, paid £10,000 annually to the Treasurer of Calais, until 1502. After that date the sum varied from £5,000 to £7,700. The Treasurer also received £2,500–£3,000 from other sources; but he always had a surplus of income over expenditure, ranging from £500 to £6,000.

Whenever troops were needed on a large scale, Henry would send out commissions of array to the leading nobility and gentry in the counties, ordering them to provide men for his service. Such men were likely to be untrained, poorly armed and ill-disciplined, and could hardly be compared with the professional armies maintained by the kings of France and Spain. To quote Pickthorn again, 'Henry VII was stronger than any of his predecessors to enforce his will throughout his dominions on condition that his will was actively shared by the prosperous and passively shared, or at least not actively resented, by the masses: conditions which on the whole he fulfilled without difficulty' (**31,** p. 77).

5 Parliament

In Henry VII's England government was essentially a matter for the king and his Council. Parliament was neither an integral nor a regular part of this machinery. The king called it as and when he wished, and Henry claimed credit for the fact that his parliaments were infrequent and that his subjects were thereby saved the expense of paying for their representatives to make constant visits to Westminster. Henry reigned for twenty-four years, but during this time he met only seven parliaments, of which five took place in the first ten years of the reign. As he grew richer and more settled on the throne he had less need for a representative body, and if the concept of parliament had depended for survival solely on its frequency, this institution would have gone the way of its French counterpart. All but three of Henry's parliaments met for one session only, lasting a few weeks at most, and second sessions, when they did take place, were as shortlived as first ones. The total time taken up by meetings in the period from 1485 to 1509 was sixty-nine weeks—just under three weeks for each year of the reign (**15**).

THE LORDS

Parliament was still primarily what it had been in the Middle Ages, a meeting of the king and his councillors with the peers of the realm. The Commons took little direct part, and were technically onlookers at the main proceedings. The lords met in a room in the royal palace at Westminster, where they were grouped, appropriately enough, around a throne. The king himself frequently presided at meetings, and when he was absent his place was taken by his closest servant, the Lord Chancellor. Near the throne sat the judges and other members of the Council, but they were there technically as advisers, and took no part in debates or voting. This does not mean that the role of the councillors was purely formal. The judges were of particular importance, since parliament was a high court and they were experts in the law, whose advice was essential when it came to the phrasing of a statute or a decision about the competence of parliament itself to deal with certain matters. But apart from the judges and a few other officials, councillors who were not themselves noble had no active role in these assemblies, and many of them preferred to stand for election to the so-called lower House—a sign that the centre of political power was shifting.

The lords consisted of two estates, the spiritual and the secular. Only thirteen archbishops and bishops and seventeen abbots and priors came to the first parliament of Henry's reign, but in a full house the spiritual peers totalled just under fifty. The lay lords were much fewer in number at the beginning of the reign, and only eighteen were present at Henry's first parliament. This was partly because of attainders, but was primarily due to the fact that the heads of many noble houses were minors—the result of natural causes, intensified by the Wars of the Roses. As the reign progressed, minors came of age, attainders were reversed, and five new peerages were created. Henry did not feel bound to summon every peer to a meeting of Parliament, but even so the number of lay peers actually present increased until it was about forty. This still left the lay peers in the minority, and Henry—a conventionally devout man, whose relations with the church were, on the whole, excellent—could rely on the spiritual peers for support of his measures.

The king and his Council and the peers of the realm made up between them a *magnum concilium*, and the presence of the Commons was not essential to this body. There seem to have been about five or six of these *magna concilia* during Henry's reign, but their competence, and therefore their usefulness, was limited. Generally speaking, the *magnum concilium* was turning into the House of Lords—although this term was not used until the closing years of Henry VIII's reign—since king, lords and Commons could do between them what no other body could do.

THE COMMONS

The Commons were already a House, both in fact and in current phraseology, by the time Henry VII came to the throne, since they had to be called something to distinguish them from the lords who

49

were parliament. While the lords and the king discussed affairs of state in the royal palace, the Commons met in the nearby chapter-house of the Abbey of Westminster. If Henry had anything of particular importance to say, he might well summon the Commons to appear before him—as he did in his first parliament, in order to give them a lecture on his right to the throne of England. But generally speaking the Commons took no part in the business of parliament, except at the beginning and end, when they squeezed into cramped positions at one end of the room (technically outside it) in which the king and his lords were debating, and made a report of their proceedings through the mouth of their Speaker.

The choice of Speaker was made by the Commons themselves, who elected one of their own number, but by the time Henry VII ascended the throne it was already accepted that the Commons' choice would be determined by the king. It is not certain how exactly the king made it known whom he wished to be elected to this key position, but all the Speakers of the reign (of whom the first was Thomas Lovell) were royal nominees. The Speaker was paid by the king, often liberally, and was responsible not only for reporting the proceedings of the lower House to the lords assembled in parliament, but also for guiding those proceedings and making sure that the will of his royal master was not blocked. In other words, some of the techniques of management which Elizabeth I was later so skilfully to employ had already been developed under the first Tudor.

Until 1544 the Speakers were chosen from among the knights of the shire, who had, as a group, a certain pre-eminence in the lower House. Two knights were elected for each of the thirty-seven shires by freeholders who held land to the value of at least forty shillings a year, and because they were men of high social standing and independence the knights took a leading part in the organisation and business of the lower House, even though they were in a minority. The majority of members—222 in Henry VII's reign—sat for boroughs, and were elected on a variety of franchises, in which the only common element was the importance of the merchant oligarchy which controlled most towns. Not all the burgesses in the House of Commons were townsmen. The process had already started by which local landowners sometimes put themselves forward as candidates for election to a borough seat, often holding out the inducement of paying their own expenses, if they were elected, instead of demanding, as they had a legal right to do, that the constituency should pay them. Members of the king's Council would also stand for borough seats, since they could play a much more significant part in the proceedings of the lower House than they could in those of the upper. The fact that councillors were anxious to find seats in the Commons, and that country gentlemen were sometimes willing to pay for this privilege, shows that representation was no longer generally regarded as an unwelcome burden. It also suggests that the infrequency of Parliaments, and the apparently humble role of the House of Commons, does not accurately indicate the prestige attached to membership. However little the Commons did, and however rarely they met, representation was a prize which men were prepared to struggle and pay for.

Because they were part of the High Court of Parliament, whose work must not be impeded by the processes of any inferior courts, members of the Commons had certain privileges. They could not, for instance, be arrested for debt, breach of contract, or other civil suit, while Parliament was in session. As for their discussions, if the Speaker misreported these they had the right—formally granted to them, in response to the Speaker's request, at the opening of every Parliament—to amend his report [**doc. 6**]. From this limited privilege was to develop the great claim to freedom of speech, but no such claim was ever made by the Commons of Henry VII. This does not necessarily mean that they did not dare talk freely within their own House—their debates were not, after all, recorded, and as long as the outcome of these was satisfactory the king had little need to worry about their course. Yet it would be wrong to assume that members of the Commons spoke with the degree of freedom even of their Elizabethan successors. For one thing they stood in awe of the king, and would be no more likely to criticise him inside the house than outside it. For another they approved, in general, of what Henry was doing, since the benefits of peace and good order were only too apparent to them. Short and infrequent sessions meant, in any case, that they had little time in which to develop a sense of corporate identity in opposition to the king. They were summoned for a specific purpose, namely to consent to what the king had decided, and the assumption—which they shared—was that they *would* consent. To look for evidence of a formed opposition in Henry's Commons is to read his reign through seventeenth-century spectacles.

Analysis

Even if individual members felt strongly enough about particular matters to oppose a measure, they ran the risk of incurring the royal wrath. Henry was not, of course, a member of the House of Commons, but many of his councillors were, and they acted as his eyes and ears. This is the significance of Roper's story that Thomas More, having been elected as a burgess to the parliament of 1504, dared to oppose a request for taxation, and

> made such arguments and reasons there against, that the king's demands were thereby overthrown. So that one of the king's privy chamber, named Mr Tyler, being present thereat, brought word to the king out of the Parliament House, that a beardless boy had disappointed all his purposes. Whereupon the king, conceiving great indignation towards him, could not be satisfied until he had some way revenged it. And forasmuch as he, nothing having, nothing could lose, his grace devised a causeless quarrel against his father, keeping him in the Tower until he had paid him an hundred pounds fine (**12,** p. 7).

If this story is true (see below, p. 57)—and it is worth remembering that Roper was More's son-in-law, and presumably heard it from More's own lips—it shows the sort of pressures that could be brought to bear on members of the Commons who dared oppose a measure decided on by the king. It does not necessarily imply that members were not free to express themselves; More's offence was not in speaking, but in speaking so persuasively that he overthrew the king's purposes. In any debating institution, however, the line between effective and ineffective speech is indistinct, and members must have been aware that any expression of critical opinion, even if it made no great impression, would probably be brought to the king's attention.

Henry's success in controlling parliament may be judged by the fact that he never had to veto a Bill. This was the result partly of careful management, but mainly of the identity of interest between the king and the property-owners whom he summoned to meet him. Lancastrian parliaments, and particularly the Commons, had pressed a reform programme designed to increase the efficiency of the crown rather than impede it. Members now had a monarch who was putting that reform programme into effect, and, not surprisingly, they willingly cooperated with him. Political stability was a rare blessing in late-fifteenth-century England, and it was not until towards the end of Henry VII's reign that the property-owners could begin to take it for granted and ask themselves whether they were paying too high a price.

THE FUNCTIONS OF PARLIAMENT:
1. MONEY GRANTS

Henry was not bound to summon parliament. He did so because it suited his purpose and because there were certain things that could be done only in parliament. One of the big advantages of summoning representatives of the community to Westminster was that the king could address, as it were, the whole nation. Every parliament was a dialogue, in which the king could learn about the state of the localities, while the representatives of those localities could find out what measures of the government would affect them, and in what way. When members returned to their constituencies they were expected to act not simply as journalists, giving the news from the capital, but also as government propagandists—since, by their consent in parliament, they were committed to the support even of unpopular measures like taxes. They could also be used in a more direct fashion, as in 1495, when they were given new standards of weights and measures to take home with them and distribute in their localities.

While parliament was useful as a means of two-way communication, it was essential for the granting of money and for the making of statute law. The first parliament of the reign, which met in 1485, granted Henry tunnage and poundage, on wool, woolfells and leather, for the rest of his life [**doc. 8**]. This particular indirect tax had originally been intended for the defence of the kingdom, and the grant to Henry was made 'in especial for the safeguard and keeping of the sea,' but in fact there was no check on how the king used the sums so obtained. Earlier grants had been made for specific purposes and for a limited time, but Richard III had been voted tunnage and poundage for the duration of his reign, and the similar generous treatment of Henry VII established a precedent that was not challenged until the accession of Charles I. The advantage of tunnage and poundage was that—like customs, which belonged to Henry as king—its value increased as trade flourished, and Henry's success in restoring ordered conditions and promoting commerce was directly rewarded by a larger income from this source.

In spite of the grant of tunnage and poundage, Henry was short of money in the early years of his reign. He had contracted debts as an exile which had to be repaid, and even after his accession he was forced to spend heavily on defending his position against pretenders. In 1486 and 1489 he sent commissioners into the counties to demand loans from his richer subjects [**doc. 10**]—loans which worked out, on the average, at £1 per head—and although this method of raising money seems crude to modern eyes, it was successful and apparently aroused little resentment. Henry's reputation was enhanced, and his credit improved, by the fact that these forced loans, and others, were apparently all repaid.

Forced loans had the advantage that they could be levied without going to the trouble of summoning parliament, and that they did not have to justified by war or the threat of war. Henry, like Edward IV before him, aimed to 'live of his own' and not to trouble his subjects except in case of necessity; but war was generally regarded as justifying parliamentary taxation, and in 1487 parliament was summoned to provide money for the suppression of Simnel's rising. It voted two fifteenths and tenths—the first direct tax of the reign—as well as a graduated poll-tax on foreign traders. In theory fifteenths and tenths were levies on personal property, but since the reign of Edward III they had become increasingly stereotyped, and now represented a sum of a little under £30,000, made up by fixed contributions from every parish. The advantage of this was obvious from the point of view of those who voted the taxes. They knew exactly what they were committing themselves to, and the fact that the obligation of every locality had been fixed by time-honoured custom kept criticism and resistance to a minimum. They also profited from the fact that a standardised grant took no account of increased wealth, and that where, as had happened in many cases, the burden of taxation fell most heavily on those who were least able to afford it, the richer section of society could continue to enjoy its built-in benefit.

The crown, on the other hand, appreciated the need for a more flexible system, and throughout the period of Lancastrian rule the Exchequer had tried a number of experiments to bring taxation into a closer relation with income and real wealth. This attempt was renewed in 1489, when parliament voted £100,000 to help the king in his struggle to stop France from swallowing the duchy of Brittany (see p. 82). Three-quarters of this sum was to be raised by the laity, through an income tax of ten per cent and a levy on personal property. The assessment was to be made by royal commissioners, sent into the counties for this specific purpose. This experiment was, in fact, the prototype of the subsidy, the main tax of Tudor England after Henry VII, but in this early form it was a failure. For one thing the royal commissioners set the sums too low, either from inexperience or from reluctance to tax themselves and their fellow property-owners too heavily, so that by autumn a mere £18,000 had been collected. And, for another, the novelty of the tax caused widespread disturbance, particularly among the poor, who regarded it as a device to squeeze yet more money out of them. Anger flared into rebellion in the north of England, where the Earl of Northumberland, acting—most uncharacteristically for a Percy—as a royal tax-collector, was killed in a brawl at Thirsk (see p. 43). The rebels went on to attack York, and Henry only restored order after he had called out the army. Taxation levied at this cost was likely to be self-defeating, and parliament had to vote a conventional fifteenth and tenth to make up the deficit. But Henry was not prepared to abandon the subsidy. The experiment was repeated in 1497 and 1504, and on both occasions was comparatively successful, yielding more than £30,000.[1]

Two years later, in July 1491, when Anne of Brittany called on Henry for wholehearted support, the king demanded a benevolence from his richer subjects and corporations. A benevolence (so-called because it was supposedly granted out of the *benevolentia* or goodwill of the giver) differed from a forced loan in that it was regarded as a gift, not to be repaid [**doc. 24**]. The main advantage of it from the king's point of view was speedy collection and the fact that, since it did not affect the poorer elements in society, it was not likely to lead to rioting. It might be thought that those who paid the benevolence would have resented it, but the 1495 parliament—

---

[1] These figures are based on an unpublished Ph.D. Thesis by R. S. Schofield 'Parliamentary Lay Taxation 1485–1547' in the Cambridge University Library. According to this the yields for Henry VII's reign were as follows:

Lay	Subsidies	Fifteenths and Tenths			
1488	£571	1488	£29,072	1492 (II)	£27,011
1489	£18,300	1489	£29,405	1497 (I)	£29,266
1497	£30,088	1490–91	£28,861	1497 (II)	£29,252
1504	£30,873	1492 (I)	£29,300		

which, like all Tudor parliaments, was an assembly representative of the richer sections of English society—gave its implicit approval to benevolences, despite the fact that they had been declared illegal in a statute of Richard III's reign, by authorising Henry to collect any sums outstanding. It may be that members recognised the justice of Henry's claim that they, having more, should contribute more; or perhaps they calculated that if they cooperated with the king in this respect, he would not be driven to fleece them in other ways.

Parliament's general approval of Henry's foreign policy was demonstrated in October 1491, when two fifteenths and tenths were voted, with the promise of a third if the English army had to spend a long time campaigning on the continent [**doc. 14**]. Five years later Henry needed money to protect his kingdom against the Scots, and decided to demand a loan. He first summoned a *magnum concilium*, to which certain burgesses and merchants were also invited. This hybrid body 'granted' the king £120,000, and with this demonstration of support to aid them, the royal commissioners were able to raise loans amounting to just under half that sum. In January of the following year, 1497, a full parliament assembled, and whatever its feelings may have been towards the earlier bastard assembly, it turned the previous 'grant'—which had been no more, in actual fact, than an expression of goodwill—into a cash reality, by voting two fifteenths and tenths to cover the king's past expenses, and a further 'aid and subsidy of as great and large sums of money as the said two fifteenths and tenths . . . should have amounted to'. This was heavy taxation by the standards of early-Tudor England, and it drove the Cornishmen—who could not see why they should have to pay hard-earned money for the defence of far-distant and alien northerners—into revolt (see p. 87).

Henry made only one more demand for direct taxation after this date, partly because he had established himself firmly on the throne and was daily becoming richer, and partly because he kept out of expensive foreign wars and entanglements. The final demand came in 1504, when the king asked for the payment of two feudal aids, one for the knighting of his eldest son, and the other for the marriage of his eldest daughter. The legality of such demands could not be contested, even though Prince Arthur had been knighted fifteen years earlier, and had been two years in his tomb in 1504; while the marriage of Princess Margaret to the King of

Scotland had taken place in 1503. Feudal aids, however, as distinct from feudal incidents, demanded the assent of those who were called upon to pay them, and Henry therefore summoned parliament. According to Roper, he asked for three fifteenths (about £45,000) and would have got this sum but for the intervention of Thomas More (see p. 52). In fact the Commons eventually offered a subsidy of £40,000, and Henry was graciously pleased to accept only £30,000; but although Roper may have got the details of his story wrong, it seems very likely that there was opposition to Henry's demands. Feudal aids could be levied only from those who held on feudal tenures, but a detailed investigation into such tenures might open the way to a further increase in the exaction of wardship and other feudal incidents. The landowners in the Commons preferred to pay up rather than have their tenures examined, but it may well be that Henry—who was not short of money by this time—had originally intended to commit parliament to accept just such an examination, and that More, by playing on the fears of the property-owners in the Commons, had deprived the king of this opportunity. This would certainly account for Henry's anger.

THE FUNCTIONS OF PARLIAMENT:
2. STATUTE LAW

If Parliament's existence had depended solely upon its exclusive right to control taxation, it would have ended after the first ten years or so of Henry's reign, when the king was not simply out of debt but was beginning to accumulate a reserve of treasure. But parliament had one other important function which it alone could perform, namely the making of statute law. Statute was the highest form of law and had the enormous advantage that, unlike royal proclamations, it was enforceable in the courts of common law. In the late-fifteenth and early-sixteenth century there was increasing emphasis in Europe upon the rights of the ruler and the duty of the subject to obey, yet in England, at any rate, it remained true that the king's powers were limited by the common law. Although he appointed the judges, who held office only during his pleasure, and although he could insist that when any case concerned him closely he should be consulted before it was continued with, he could not change the law which was administered in the courts unless he obtained the consent of the lords and Commons in parliament. This limitation on the king's authority was not, in fact, a great handicap, since the common law maintained the property rights of the king (the greatest of all property-owners) as well as those of his subjects, and in the last resort, as the reign of Charles I was to show, the common law could not bind the king when he invoked his prerogative powers. Yet it remains true that in Henry VII's England the highest form of law was not that which issued from the king's own mouth, but that which he made with the advice and assent of the upper section of English society.

The assumption that law is something higher than the mere wishes of the men who make it is shown by the so-called 'De Facto' Act of 1495. This was designed to protect all those who served the king from possible revenge by a successful usurper, and declared that anyone who should 'attend upon the king and sovereign lord of this land for the time being in his person, and do him true and faithful service of allegiance in the same . . . be in no wise convict or attaint of high treason nor of other offences for that cause, by act of Parliament or otherwise by any process of law'. The principle of this statute—that men should not be punished for their loyalty—is unexceptionable, though Henry himself had shown no awareness of it in his treatment of defeated Yorkists; but its tone is peculiar to modern ears, since it seems to be stating a moral principle under the form of legislative enactment. This impression is reinforced by the last section of the statute, which declared that 'if any act or acts or other process of the law hereafter thereupon for the same happen to be made contrary to this ordinance, that then that act or acts or other processes of the law, whatsoever they shall be, stand and be utterly void'. The assumption that parliament can bind its successors shows the difference in attitude towards the law between the early Tudor period and that of our own day. Law was something to be revealed rather than created, and once a principle of justice had been laid bare it could not, in the nature of things, be changed. In fact, as parliament came to make more and more law, its attitude altered, but in the reign of Henry VII, at any rate, parliament regarded itself as the guardian rather than the maker of law.

Although Henry summoned parliaments only rarely, he made considerable use of statute to carry out his policies. Altogether there were about 120 public Acts passed during his reign, and the average number per session is about the same as under Henry VIII. Many government measures made their first appearance in the Commons, and although members could and did continue to put forward public Bills of their own—Bills, that is, which affected the interest of the country as a whole, and not simply that of an individual or corporation—an increasing number of Bills, even though they took the form of requests from the Commons, were inspired by the king and his ministers. It is not always possible, however, to distinguish between government proposals and those which really sprang from the Commons: this is especially true of social and economic measures, in which the Commons had a particular interest, and it may well be that many of the penal statutes from which Henry profited—by collecting fines for infringement—were the result of Commons' pressures rather than of his own cunning schemes for increasing royal revenue.

One of the major functions of parliament was the strengthening of the crown, and the first parliament of the reign declared for the 'avoiding of all ambiguities and questions' that 'the inheritance of the crowns of the realms of England and of France, with all the pre-eminence and dignity royal to the same pertaining, and all other seigniories to the king belonging beyond the sea . . . be, rest, remain and abide in the most royal person of our now sovereign lord king Henry the VIIth and in the heirs of his body lawfully coming' [**doc. 5**]. There was no question, of course, of a parliamentary title. Henry was king by right—or so at least he claimed, and parliament did not care to dispute this. Their object in recognising his title was simply to make sure that it could not be challenged in the courts, and that Henry should have full possession of all the lands which belonged to the crown. The 'De Facto' Act of 1495 was another measure designed to strengthen the crown by encouraging men to serve it wholeheartedly, without constantly looking over their shoulders to see if a pretender was on the horizon.

There was one further way in which parliament reinforced Henry's position. This was by striking down his enemies by acts of attainder, which transferred their property to the crown [**doc. 13**]. Acts of attainder had been used frequently during the Wars of the Roses to cripple adherents of the defeated side, and Henry opened his reign with a batch of attainders against prominent Yorkists. There was some opposition in the Commons to this [**doc. 7**], possibly

59

because members felt that attainders were a threat to all property rights, their own included, and one member reported that 'there was many gentlemen against it. But it would not be, for it was the king's pleasure'. The second parliament of the reign saw twenty-eight attainders, following the suppression of the Simnel conspiracy, and Henry kept up this heavy pressure upon his opponents even after he had become firmly established on the throne. His last parliament, in 1504, passed more acts of attainder than any of the others, and only the parliament of 1497 was entirely free of them.

Parliament was concerned not only with reinforcing Henry's hold on the throne, but also with strengthening the executive, thereby encouraging the restoration of good order to a disturbed country. The so-called 'Star Chamber' Act of 1487 listed some of the major incentives to disorder—'unlawful maintenances; giving of liveries, signs and tokens and retainders by indenture, promises, oaths, writing or otherwise; embraceries of [the king's] subjects; untrue demeanings of sheriffs in making of panels, and other untrue returns; taking of money by juries; great riots and unlawful assemblies'—and gave a committee of the Council statutory authority to enquire into these, to summon suspected evil-doers before them, and 'to punish them after their demerits' [**doc. 11**].

Members of parliament had good reason to know, however, that no amount of activity by the central government would be effective unless it were matched by increased vigour in the localities, and statutes were passed throughout the reign designed to strengthen the powers of justices of the peace. In 1485 an Act to prevent hunting under cover of darkness or in disguise gave justices of the peace authority to issue a warrant for the arrest of any person and to carry out a preliminary examination of him on suspicion alone, without waiting for formal indictment by a grand jury; and two years later it was enacted that at least two justices must be present before bail could be granted to an offender. In 1495 justices of the peace were authorised to hear and determine, without indictment by a jury, all offences short of felony. They were also required to exercise control and supervision over local officials, and to watch over, and if necessary amend, jury panels which had been appointed by the sheriffs to enquire into the king's rights [**doc. 18**].

A number of statutes strengthened the powers of justices of the peace to deal with riots, and an Act of 1504 required them to order the sheriffs to appoint special juries of landowners to present all cases of livery and retainer known to, or suspected by, them. These jurors were to be men of substance, and the principle of relying on the wealthier elements in English society to cooperate with the king in restoring order was shown in another Act, requiring that all London jurors should be men of property. The poor were not neglected. In 1495 the Chancellor was authorised to grant them free writs and counsel, and the statute of 1489 (see p. 46) laid down the procedure they could use in case justices of the peace were negligent in attending to their complaints. But in general Henry enlisted the support of the property-holders, because they shared with him the desire for order in English society, and because he had no alternative means of enforcing his will.

Henry also used parliament to bring corporations and franchises more closely under his control. Statutes were passed regulating the town governments of Northampton and Leicester; and in 1495 the franchise of Tynedale was annexed to the shire administration. Even a great and proud corporation like London was brought to heel. In 1487 a statute annulled the City ordinances forbidding citizens to take their goods to fairs and markets outside London, and ten years later parliament stepped in to stop the Merchant Adventurers of London from monopolising the valuable cloth trade of the country by imposing a high entrance fee for membership of their company. This was followed by an Act of 1504 in which it was laid down that 'no masters, wardens and fellowships of crafts . . . nor any rulers of gilds or fraternities, take upon them to make any acts or ordinances nor to execute any acts or ordinances by them heretofore made . . . but if the same acts or ordinances be examined and approved by the Chancellor, Treasurer of England, and Chief Justices of either Bench'. Henry in fact had little trouble with corporations, but these statutes emphasised the principle that all jurisdictional and legislative rights derived from the crown, and could, if necessary, be controlled or even resumed. This was part of the process of centralising government which Henry VIII was to accelerate and extend.

The principle of centralisation was also applied by parliament in matters which affected the country's economy, since local variations in standards hindered trade. Acts were passed to improve the coinage and to establish uniform weights and measures, and members were urged to see that these were carried into effect. Attempts were also made to control the movement of the economy.

61

Analysis

In 1489, for instance, came the first general statute against depopulation and eviction; and in 1485 and 1489 Navigation Acts were passed, with the aim of promoting the shipping industry, and through it the navy (see p. 75).

Other measures were concerned with social discipline, such as the act of 1495 which laid down maximum wage rates and minimum hours of work, and forbade the witholding of labour.[1] Another act of this year dealt with the poor, by ordering that vagabonds found in towns should be put in the stocks and then expelled, while beggars were to be returned to their own hundred. Behind much of this legislation may be discerned fear—fear that labourers might combine to demand higher wages and shorter hours of work; fear that the unemployed might accumulate in the towns, providing fodder for rebellion. Fear may also be discerned behind a number of statutes for licensing trade and imposing certain standards. In these cases the fear was that if the operation of the economy was left entirely alone, some trades and industries would attract too many participants, thereby reducing the level of profit and encouraging unscrupulous men to defraud customers by lowering the quality of their goods. The statutes concerned with licensing were usually 'penal'—that is, they encouraged the use of informers, and provided that in the case of a successful prosecution the profits should be shared between the informer and the king. These statutes were of considerable benefit to the king, but they became associated with some of the more unpleasant features of Henry's government, and were to that extent responsible for the revulsion against his methods which found expression as soon as his son came to the throne.

Parliament's concern for social discipline led it into the frontier land between Church and State. Benefit of clergy, originally designed to protect clerics from judgment by lay courts, had turned into an abuse, since anyone who could read could claim this right and thereby escape punishment—except by the mild censures of the Church. In 1489, therefore, a statute ordered that benefit of clergy should be confined to those who were actually in holy orders. Those who could merely read were to have benefit once, and once only. To make sure that they could never claim it a second time, they were to be branded. The justification for this legislation was that it

[1] The provisions affecting wages were repealed in the following year.

concerned law and order, which was the particular province of parliament. It seems to have aroused little or no protest from the rulers of the church. For one thing the Pope himself had recognised the abuse of benefit of clergy and had issued a bull to restrain it; and, for another, Henry's relations with Rome and with the church in England were so good [**doc. 16**] that his actions were regarded in the most favourable light. As for parliament, it made no attempt in this reign to trespass on spiritual matters. Although in some ways it acted as a supreme lawgiver, it also recognised implicit limits upon its freedom of action. The big extension of parliamentary competence did not come until after 1529.

6 The Economy

ENCLOSURES

The economy of England in Henry VII's reign was based upon agriculture, most of which was for subsistence. Apart from food, the most important single commodity was wool, which formed the basis of England's major industry and accounted for some ninety per cent of English exports. The demand for wool had a marked effect upon the pattern of English farming, since many farmers found it more profitable to turn their estates over to sheep than to continue to cultivate them in the traditional manner. This affected the rural community in three main ways: enclosure, engrossing and depopulation—an unholy trinity which came to be the bugbear of Tudor governments. These three did not always take place at one and the same time, nor were the terms used precisely: enclosure, for instance, was not necessarily accompanied by depopulation, but it was often used simply as an expression of hostile opinion.

Enclosure meant the fencing-off of a man's property, and the extinguishing of common rights over it, so that it could be cultivated without reference to the community. There were innumerable ways of carrying this out, ranging from high-handed action by a single landlord to joint agreement by the occupiers of an estate. It could be carried out in the open fields, by consolidation of strips, in the common pasture, or in the waste land that extended beyond a village. The advantage of enclosure was that it enabled the progressive farmer to develop his own techniques, without being held back by the inability, conservatism or laziness of his neighbours. In particular, it enabled him to go in for selective breeding of animals, especially sheep, in order to improve the quality of his stock. The main objection to enclosure was that it might well lead to the eviction of families which had settled in the affected area without ever acquiring definite legal rights. Freeholders could claim a share of the land to be enclosed (though they were sometimes too supine to defend their rights); copyholders also had a claim, which could be enforced in Chancery and the prerogative courts if the common law courts (which were, in fact, beginning to take cognisance of copyholds during Henry's reign) refused to act. But tenants-at-will, cottagers and squatters were unprotected except by custom, and, if they were evicted, had nowhere to go.

Engrossing meant the throwing-together of a number of fields or farms in order to make a more efficient unit. In this case one set of farm buildings might be abandoned and the tenants evicted. This could happen on a larger scale, where a landlord might decide to get rid of an entire village and turn the land over to sheep and a single shepherd. It was this depopulation—which usually, though not necessarily, accompanied engrossing of holdings, and was often a feature of enclosure—that caused resentment, unrest and therefore official concern. Tudor governments objected to depopulation on moral grounds, but they were driven to take action by the fear that unemployed vagrants, many of whom flocked into the towns, would be fuel for rebellion as well as carriers of disease, and that the 'sturdy peasantry' upon which the nation depended for its defence would be gravely depleted.

Enclosures—using this term in a general sense—were a frequent cause of riots in Henry VII's reign. At Coventry, for instance, in 1496, the rich burgesses of the town council decided to enclose the Lammas fields on which many of the inhabitants grazed their sheep and cattle. The opposition to this move was led by one of the townsmen, who organised his supporters and distributed propaganda, containing rhymes such as the one which started

> 'The city is bond that should be free.
> The right is holden from the commonalty.
> Our commons, that at Lammas open should be cast,
> They be closed in and hedged full fast.' (**13**, vol. 3, p. 13)

As far as the destruction of villages was concerned, most of the damage had been done before Henry VII came to the throne, but his government was sufficiently alarmed to pass the first legislation against this practice. An Act of 1489 was specifically directed to the Isle of Wight, essential to the nation's defence, where conversion of arable to pasture and engrossing had rendered the Island 'desolate and not inhabited, but occupied with beasts and cattle'. The same year also saw a general Act which, while it makes no mention of enclosure, recites how 'great inconveniences daily doth increase by desolation and pulling-down and wilful waste of houses and towns within this . . . realm, and laying to pasture lands which customably have been used in tilth', and complains that 'where in some towns two hundred persons were occupied and lived by their lawful labours, now be there occupied two or three herdsmen'. The only remedy provided by the Act was an order that all towns and houses should in future be maintained—a pious hope, but not very effective in halting the economic forces which were transforming the countryside.

The impact of enclosures was limited, in the main, to the midland area of England. Outside this area some places, like Kent, had never known the strip system, while others—like the greater part of Essex, Suffolk, Hertfordshire, Devon, Somerset, Cornwall, Shropshire, Worcestershire and Herefordshire—had been wholly enclosed before 1500. Where pasture was abundant enclosures could be carried through without too much dispute over grazing rights, and certain types of soil were, of course, better suited to the cultivation of sheep or cattle than of corn. Enclosure was sometimes carried out by agreement, and if it was unaccompanied by depopulation it might pass without protest. But in the midland counties, where population was increasing rapidly, the requirements of efficient farming often conflicted with the interests of the community—and particularly of its poorer members. In many areas all the waste land between village and village was taken into cultivation (a process that was often accompanied by bitter disputes over village boundaries), but even this did not ease the pressure of population. More families meant more cattle and sheep on the common pastures, and made communal grazing rights in the open fields, after harvest, even more valuable and highly prized. Farmers who wanted to profit from the increased demand for wool, meat and dairy products, could do so only by exceeding the limitation ('stint') placed upon the number of animals they could graze, or by enclosing their property, thereby reducing the amount of grazing available to their neighbours.

Enclosure and engrossing were unfortunately often accompanied by depopulation, and where this was so, the cost in human suffering was high. When the landlords, lay or clerical, owned most of the manor they could simply tell the peasant farmers to leave after the harvest had been gathered in, pull their cottages down, and sow the strips with grass. Some of the grazing areas created by such methods

66

were very large: one made by a Leicestershire priory in 1494 covered more than 400 acres. Although Henry VII's government, like that of his successors, was formally opposed to depopulating enclosures, some of the chief offenders were themselves officers of the household. At Wormleighton, for instance, on the borders of Warwickshire and Northamptonshire, William Cope, Cofferer of the Household, evicted the inhabitants of twelve farms and three cottages in October 1498, enclosed 240 acres of arable with hedges and ditches, and turned the newly created fields over to sheep and cattle. Sixty persons lost their dwellings as a result of this particular operation.

WOOL AND CLOTH

The obverse of this gloomy picture is the prosperity of the trade in wool and woollen cloth, and of the towns and villages which thrived on it. The clothier was a familiar figure in Henry VII's England, riding round the country buying wool, arranging for its collection and distribution to the centres where it could either be packed for export or else woven into cloth. The main centres of cloth manufacture were the Midlands and East Anglia, and great perpendicular churches, like those at Long Melford and Lavenham, testify to the wealth of the clothiers as well as to their piety, and to the prosperity of small towns which could afford to erect and maintain these cathedral-like buildings.

Most of the clothiers were Englishmen, but there were a number of foreign buyers, and jealousy towards them is shown by an Act of 1489 forbidding them to negotiate for wool until native Englishmen had already completed their transactions. The Act also forbade the buying of wool for manufacture outside England, but this attempt to stimulate the already thriving industry was not rigidly enforced. In fact exports of raw wool had been declining before Henry VII came to the throne, because of the heavy taxation to which they were subject, as well as the increasing demand of the native cloth industry. This decline continued throughout Henry's reign, and by 1509 wool exports were some thirty per cent lower than they had been in 1485. This affected the merchants of the Staple, who had a monopoly of the export of raw wool to Calais, the staple town, and were financially responsible for the maintenance of the garrison there. But while the trade in raw wool was shrinking, the export of cloth was flourishing, and sixty per cent more cloth was being sent abroad by the end of Henry's reign than had been exported in the early years. Henry, of course, actively encouraged the development of this trade. His own wealth and that of his kingdom stood to gain by it, and in addition wool affected so many people—from the merchants who traded in it to the landlords who reared the sheep; and from the housewives who spun it to the shepherds and shearers who provided the raw material—that prosperity would encourage acceptance of Henry and his dynasty. One of the reasons for the Yorkist sympathies of London and smaller wool towns had been the feebleness of Lancastrian foreign policy: Henry was aware that by encouraging trade abroad he would be strengthening his position at home.

The leading part in cloth export was taken by the Merchant Adventurers. These were not confined to London—there were the Merchant Adventurers of Bristol, for instance—but the London company was far and away the most important of its kind, and dominated the trade with Antwerp. The trouble with the London Adventurers was that they wished to establish a monopoly of all cloth exports, and this was resented by the merchants of the 'outports'—particularly towns like Bristol and Boston. The London company took the first step towards establishing a monopoly in 1496, when it declared that anyone trading in cloth should pay a fine of £20 to it. This was a prohibitively high sum, designed to keep the numbers of people involved in the trade small, so that profits would be correspondingly big. Such high-handed action brought the company up against parliament, where the Londoners were in a minority, and an Act of the following year condemned the Adventurers' action as springing from 'their uncharitable and inordinate covetousness for their singular profit and lucre' and declared that the only effects had been to drive merchants away from the trade, 'whereby the woollen cloth of this realm, which is one of the great commodities of the same, by making whereof the king's true subjects be put in occupation, and the poor people have most universally their living . . . is not sold nor uttered as it hath been in time past'. The Merchant Adventurers were accordingly commanded to cut their prohibitive entrance fee by two-thirds, and their aggressiveness was again checked in 1504, after disputes between them and the Staplers, whom they had been forcibly trying to take over, when a decree of the Council in Star Chamber ordered each company to respect the privileges and scope of the other.

While Henry was willing to restrain the Merchant Adventurers at home, for fear that they should constrict trade instead of expanding it, he gave them full support abroad. In 1505 a royal charter authorised the company to inspect cloth and maintain minimum standards of quality, and also to settle disputes and take whatever other measures were necessary for the efficient functioning of the trade. The Adventurers' entrance fee was fixed at £5, the implication being that they would be given a virtual monopoly of cloth exports on condition that they did not attempt to confine membership to an oligarchy of rich men.

The main outlet for the sale of English cloth was Antwerp, which was rapidly becoming the commercial capital of Europe. To Antwerp came spices and rich fabrics from the east; naval stores and corn from the Baltic; silver and other metals from Germany; Mediterranean produce from Spain; and hides, tin and pewter—as well as cloth—from England. While English merchants depended upon Antwerp for easy sale of their cloth, since buyers were present there from all over Europe, they were not necessarily bound to it. Cloth was so important a commodity that buyers would follow wherever the market moved. The factories of Flanders, on the other hand, which specialised in taking the coarse cloth, refining it, and turning it into a variety of fabrics, could not be moved, and this fact gave Henry a weapon which he did not hesitate to use. In 1493, when the ruler of the Netherlands was giving support to the pretender Perkin Warbeck, Henry ordered the Merchant Adventurers to join the Staplers at Calais, and an embargo on trade with the Netherlands remained in force until 1496. The Netherlands put a counter-embargo on the import of English goods, and although the trade upon which both countries had based their wealth did not dry up completely, it was irregular and restricted. Neither side stood to gain much from this embargo, and a return to sanity was signalised by the signing of the *Magnus Intercursus* in 1496, which Professor Wernham has called 'the Magna Carta of the English traders' position in the Netherlands' (**35**, p. 68). Under the terms of this agreement, English merchants were free to sell their goods wholesale anywhere in the Duke of Burgundy's dominions except Flanders itself, and were guaranteed swift and fair justice; a regular machinery for the settlement of disputes, inspection of goods, and recovery of debts; and security against any new tolls or duties.

There is no evidence that the *Magnus Intercursus* resulted in any appreciable increase in the volume of English cloth sales to the Netherlands, but it provided a foundation upon which good commercial relations could be—and were—built. The Merchant Adventurers could not, of course, sit back and enjoy their privileges. The ink was hardly dry on the agreement before Philip of Burgundy imposed a new import duty on English cloth, and Henry sent the Adventurers back to Calais again. In July 1497 Philip agreed that the new duty should be removed, and Henry consented that in return the Adventurers should abandon their right to sell freely in the Netherlands and confine themselves to Antwerp and Bergen-op-Zoom. The merchants, however, were not prepared to accept any such limitation, and refused to move from Calais. They stayed there until May 1499, when Philip confirmed the *Magnus Intercurcus* and the normal pattern of trade was restored.

More disputes between the Netherlands government and the Merchant Adventurers came to a head in 1504, when Henry once again shifted the cloth staple to Calais, and later imposed a complete embargo on trade between England and the Low Countries. His bargaining position was enormously strengthened when, in 1506, Philip was forced by a violent gale to abandon his projected journey to Spain and to run for shelter to the nearest English port [**doc. 26**]. Once in England he became the guest of Henry VII, who invited him to Windsor, showered hospitality and attentions upon him, and got him to agree to a commercial treaty in which English merchants were given the right to sell wholesale everywhere within the duke's dominions, and retail anywhere except Flanders. The name given by Bacon to this agreement—*Malus Intercursus*—is accurate enough, since instead of being based, like the *Magnus Intercursus*, on principles that would give the maximum benefit to both sides, it was extorted by Henry out of Philip's weakness, and gave the English merchants in the Netherlands such a privileged position that the nominal benefits were likely to be outweighed by the resentment they caused. In fact the treaty, which was followed shortly by Philip's death, never really became operative, and in 1507 another agreement confirmed the *Magnus Intercursus* as the basis for trading relations between the two countries.

THE EXPANSION OF OVERSEAS TRADE

While Henry encouraged the vital trade between England and the Netherlands, he also used diplomacy to increase the share of English merchants in other markets, no doubt aware that by so doing he was reducing the dependence upon one outlet which, in times of crisis, could be a weakness. There was quite a flourishing trade in existence between France and England, based on wine from Gascony and woad from Toulouse, and the Navigation Acts of 1485 and 1489 (see p. 75) were designed to give English ships a commanding position in this. In 1486 Henry signed a commercial agreement with France, removing the restrictions that had hampered Anglo-French trade since the days of Edward IV. But the quarrel over Brittany, with which Henry had also made a treaty of commerce, led the French to reimpose the restrictions on English merchants, and these remained in force until Henry came to terms with the king of France at Etaples in 1492. Even then they were only moderated. Not until 1495 were they entirely swept away—part of the price that France had to pay for English neutrality during the Italian wars—and in 1497 a new treaty of commerce confirmed the privileges of English merchants trading with the King of France's dominions.

Further south Henry renewed in 1489, the treaty of friendship with Portugal, concluded over a hundred years earlier. He also took steps to increase the part played by English merchants in trade with Spain. Edward IV had granted special privileges to Spanish merchants, which enabled them to dominate Anglo-Spanish trade and even cut in on that between England and France. By the commercial clauses of the treaty of Medina del Campo, however, signed in 1489, it was agreed that English and Spanish merchants should have reciprocal rights in each others' countries, and that duties should be fixed at low rates. English merchants gradually began to increase their share of Anglo-Spanish trade, particularly after the Navigation Acts. These were so effective that Spain retaliated with Navigation Acts of her own, forbidding the export of goods from Spain in foreign ships when native ones were available. With trade confined in one direction to Spanish ships, and in the other to English ones, the volume decreased, and although English merchants were more firmly entrenched in Anglo-Spanish trade at the end of Henry's reign than they had been at the beginning, the policies of each government served only to check the expansion of commerce.

Since the middle of the fifteenth century English merchants had been pushing into the Mediterranean region, buying wines from Crete and currants from the Levant. This brought them up against Venice, which had established a virtual monopoly over trade in the eastern Mediterranean and resented this threat, however small, to the commercial wealth upon which her greatness was based. The Venetians therefore imposed a heavy duty on wines taken from Venetian possessions in foreign ships, hoping thereby to preserve the privileged position of their own galleys, which made annual journeys to Europe, with Southampton as their port of call in England. Henry could not challenge Venice direct, but he could intrigue with Venice's rivals, among whom was Florence. In 1490 Henry concluded a trade treaty with Florence, and agreed that the Florentine port of Pisa should be a staple for English wool, which should be carried in English ships. Two years later he took retaliatory action against Venice by imposing a duty of eighteen shillings a butt on wines brought to England in Venetian ships. This tariff war might have continued indefinitely, without marked advantage to either side, but in 1494 came the outbreak of the Italian wars, and from then on Venice was too fully occupied at home to be able to give much attention to a commercial squabble. The tariff war died down, and by 1509 the English had built up a regular trade to Pisa and the eastern Mediterranean.

The challenge to Venice was one of the reasons which led Henry to patronise those explorers who believed that a route to the east, with its fabulous silks and spices, could be found by sailing west, thereby outflanking Venice, which dominated the established trade-routes. Henry narrowly missed becoming the patron of Columbus, but in 1496 he issued letters patent to John Cabot, authorising him 'to sail to all parts, regions and coasts of the eastern, western and northern sea'. Cabot was given a royal pension and the promise that he should have sole ownership of any new lands he discovered and a monopoly of trade with them, on condition that one-fifth of the profits went to the crown. When John Cabot returned from his first voyage of 1497, during which he discovered Newfoundland, Henry received him, listened to his story, and encouraged him to set out again the following year. John Cabot never returned from this second voyage, but Henry extended his patronage, and the pension, to John's son, Sebastian, and gave him authority to settle in any territories which were not already actually occupied by any Christian power [**doc. 25**]. In 1506 the Bristol company of 'Adventurers in the New Found Lands' was formed, which backed Sebastian's next voyage, in which he probably explored Hudson Bay and the north American coast. But by the time Sebastian returned Henry VII was dead, and with him any hope that England might join Spain and Portugal among the pioneers of exploration and settlement in the new world.

In his dealings with France, Spain and Venice, Henry was reasonably successful. In northern Europe he had a much more stubborn rival to deal with, namely the north German cities of the Hanseatic League. The Hansa merchants dominated the trade of northern Europe, and were in a highly favoured position even in England itself. They were a powerful community, very rich, and had been granted exceptional privileges by Edward IV in return for their support of him. At London, in the Steelyard, and at Southampton and Boston, they had established depots which were virtually independent republics. They could live where they pleased; they could sell certain goods retail; they were partially exempt from taxation; and the duties they paid on goods they exported were lower than those paid by English merchants.

This exceptionally privileged position inspired resentment, which Henry shared, but he had to move carefully. For one thing the Hanse could cause him a lot of trouble if it chose to support pretenders to the English throne; and, for another, England was dependent on the Hanse for a considerable part of her foreign trade, and could not afford to disrupt this. In March 1486, therefore, Henry confirmed the privileges of the Hanse in England, but he began to outflank them in other ways. An Act of parliament of the next year ordered that no aliens, including Hansards, should export unfinished cloth, and two years later they were forbidden to take money or bullion out of the country. Henry tacitly encouraged the protest of his subjects against the privileges of the Hanse. When in 1493 a London mob attacked the Steelyard [**doc. 15**], claiming that the Hansards had profited from the embargo on the trade of English merchants with the Netherlands, Henry paid little compensation, and later demanded £20,000 as security for the Hansards' promise that they would not trade with the Netherlands while any embargo was in force. The king confiscated this sum in 1508, because, he claimed, the Hansards had broken their promise. Henry also claimed that the Hansards' privilege of importing goods at a low rate of duty applied only to items originating from Hansa towns and territories, and not to those which the merchants gathered from all over Europe. When the Hanse protested, Henry refused to listen.

Henry's aim was to give English merchants direct access to the valuable Baltic market, where their woollen cloth would be welcome, and from which they could obtain essential naval stores and corn. Just as he used Florence to outflank Venice in the Mediterranean, so he used the Hanse's rivals to challenge the monopoly of the League in northern waters. In 1489 he made an alliance with Denmark, extended in 1490, which gave English merchants freedom of trade in Denmark and Norway and the right to fish in Icelandic waters. The fishing privilege, in particular, was most valuable and was taken advantage of, so that the general effect of this pressure on the Hanse was to persuade the League to come to terms. They offered to agree to the admission of English merchants to Danzig, but Danzig itself refused to accept such an agreement, and the English remained excluded. Henry then tried to take advantage of the quarrel which had broken out between Riga and the League. In 1499 a commercial treaty with Riga gave English merchants the right to trade freely there, while Rigan merchants were to have reciprocal privileges in England. Unfortunately for Henry the dispute between Riga and the League was quickly settled, and the Anglo-Rigan treaty never came into effect.

The struggle with the League continued throughout Henry's reign, except for a brief period in 1504 when Henry, in a sudden *volte-face*, confirmed the privileges of the Hanse as they had been in Edward IV's day. This otherwise inexplicable action seems to have resulted from a moment of panic when the Earl of Suffolk—the latest of the pretenders with whom Henry had to contend—fled to north Germany and looked to the League to help him. But Suffolk soon showed that Henry had nothing to fear from him, and the king returned to his old policy of whittling down the League's privileges. The Act of 1504 which confirmed the Hansards' position had included the proviso that it should not 'be in any wise prejudicial or hurtful to … the city of London', and Henry took advantage of this loophole to impose higher duties once again on the Hansa merchants. Generally speaking Henry was not very successful in his struggle against the Hanse. He managed to get England a share in the Icelandic fisheries, and he encouraged what one historian has called a 'flicker of English trade into the Baltic' (**35**, p. 73). But the League was too rich and too powerful for Henry alone to overthrow, and English shipping had not developed to the point where it could fill any vacuum that might be created by successful diplomacy.

THE ENCOURAGEMENT OF ENGLISH SHIPPING

The weakness of English shipping was part of a vicious circle. While the Hansards were available with their own ships, there was little incentive for the building of English ones; and yet, because English ships were not available, there was no possibility of an effective challenge to the Hanse. This was one of the reasons for the passing of the Navigation Acts in 1485 and 1489. The first Act, calling to mind 'the great [di]minishing and decay that hath been now of late time of the navy within this realm of England, and idleness of the mariners within the same, by the which this noble realm within short process of time, without reformation be had therein, shall not be of hability and power to defend itself', ordered that in future wines from Guienne and Gascony should be imported only in English ships, with a predominantly English crew [**doc. 9**]. The 1489 Act put the same limitation on the import of woad from Toulouse, and added a general provision that English merchants (the prohibition did not apply to aliens) should not import any goods in foreign ships when English ones were available. The outcry from the Hansa merchants, whose ships were frequently used, and the passing of similar acts by Spain, suggests that this early exercise in mercantilism was comparatively successful.

The connection between merchant shipping and naval defence was very close, since merchant vessels became warships in time of crisis. Henry needed large ships for defence, and gave a bounty to builders of vessels of more than eighty tons. During the struggle over Brittany he had had to hire ships from Spain, presumably because insufficient English ones were available, and this weakness lay behind his active encouragement of English shipbuilding. The need to employ such ships, once built, was also a further incentive to promote English commerce by diplomacy.

Edward IV had reconstructed a Royal Navy, apparently as an act of deliberate policy, after its decline during Henry VI's reign, and he used it to good purpose in his war against Scotland in 1481-82. Richard III took the same personal interest in naval matters, and had a fleet of some ten ships; but with the accession of Henry VII and the inauguration of the Tudor peace, the rate of warship construction slackened. By 1509 there were only five 'King's Ships,' but they included the *Regent* of 600 tons, which carried 225 guns, and the *Sovereign*, with 141 guns. Henry also provided the facilities which were particularly necessary for ships that were limited in range and restricted in their movement to windward. In 1495 he started construction of the navy's first dry dock, at Portsmouth; and he also developed the Thames ports, establishing arsenals at Greenwich and Woolwich. In short, while Henry could not hope to match the rulers of Europe on the battlefield, he was more than the equal of them at sea.

Henry, like Edward IV, had a personal interest in trade. He imported alum, which was essential for the making of soap, thereby infringing the papal monopoly, and made £15,000 from sales of this commodity in 1505–06. He hired out royal ships, and he also made interest-free loans to English and foreign merchants on condition that their trade benefited the customs by an agreed amount [**doc. 28**]. Customs (in which tunnage and poundage may, for convenience, be included) gave him an obvious financial interest in the state of trade. He appointed a commission to enquire into smuggling on the south coast and in the west country, but in fact smuggling does not seem to have been a major problem. He also introduced a new Book of Rates, in 1507, although this seems to have operated only in London. The yield from customs would presumably have increased without any royal encouragement, as order was restored and the population increased. But the rise of over twenty per cent in the yield, from some £33,000 in 1485 to more than £40,000 by 1509, was a considerable achievement.

It is impossible to say to what extent Henry's policy was of direct benefit to English trade. In the north his success was limited; in southern Europe it was greater. But these were minor outlets compared with the vital link between England and the Netherlands, and the volume of trade here was determined rather by reciprocal needs than conscious acts of policy. Even the proportion of this trade in the hands of alien merchants remained much the same throughout the reign. English merchants had the greater part, some fifty-three per cent; the Hanse accounted for another twenty-four per cent, and other aliens for the rest. The only conclusion that can be drawn from these figures is that without Henry's encouragement of English commerce, the share of English merchants in trade from this country might have declined. The long-term effect of his policy was perhaps more important, in that he sketched out the lines—into the Baltic, the Mediterranean, and across the Atlantic—along which English commerce was eventually to develop, and he gave it the foundation of naval power without which such development would have been impossible.

7 Foreign Policy

THE STATES OF WESTERN EUROPE

Western Europe during the period of Henry VII's reign was dominated by two great states, France and Spain, each in the process of extending its own frontiers and consolidating its central authority; and, to a lesser extent, by the somewhat shadowy authority of the Holy Roman Emperor, who was more significant as a person—and in particular as a husband and father—than as a territorial ruler.

The general tenor of French policy was in the direction of an extension of the frontiers of France to her 'natural' boundaries, although this was never consistently or consciously pursued and gained its greatest triumphs as much by accident as by design. Louis XI had been particularly successful, and by the time he died, in 1483, had nearly doubled the amount of territory held by the French crown. This was not all external gain. Part of it was at the expense of the French nobility and took place within the existing frontiers of the kingdom. He left his heir strongly placed not only in relation to his European rivals but also to those magnates whose territorial possessions limited the crown's freedom of action in much the same way as the overmighty subjects limited that of the English kings in the closing middle ages. In 1484 the Estates-General met to organise the government of the young Charles VIII, but once his power had been consolidated the king no longer summoned the representative assembly which at one time had seemed likely to acquire in France a position similar to that which parliament held in England. The king ruled through a Council that was responsible to him alone, and although the *taille*—the main direct tax—was in theory granted by the Estates-General, in fact the sum required was fixed by the royal Council and collection was carried out annually. This gave the French monarchy a source of financial strength such as Henry VII never knew.

Spain had been united only in 1479, ten years after the marriage of Ferdinand, King of Aragon, and Isabella, Queen of Castile. The southern part of the peninsula was still, however, occupied by the Moors, and Ferdinand and Isabella made it their lives' work to destroy the independence of the Moors and to reconquer the peninsula for God—and, of course, for themselves and their descendants. In this they were successful, and in 1492, just before Columbus set off on a journey that would give them a whole new world to rule, they completed the conquest of Granada. In Spain the problem of establishing central authority was much harder than in France or England, because of the different kingdoms and customs, but Ferdinand and Isabella used the same methods. They worked through a royal Council in which the nobles, although they were not deliberately excluded, were of secondary importance to officials drawn from a somewhat lower level of society; they out-lawed private war, and forbade the building of private castles; they appointed royal officials to administer the localities; and although they used the *Cortes*—the various representative assemblies—to cement their power, they made little use of them thereafter.

Ten years or so before Henry VII came to the throne of England, it looked as though Burgundy would develop into one of the major powers of Europe, but in 1477 its great duke, Charles the Bold, died, and his territories were divided. The greater part of them passed to his daughter, Mary of Burgundy, who, in 1477, married the eighteen-year-old Maximilian, Duke of Austria and heir to the Emperor Frederick III. Five years later Mary died after a riding accident, leaving a young son, Philip, to succeed to her title and her estates. Maximilian was determined to act as regent for his son, but the proud cities of the Netherlands resented what they regarded as foreign rule, and civil war continued intermittently for years, with Maximilian unable to enforce his authority. He eventually abandoned his attempt in 1493, for in that year his father died and he was elected Emperor as Maximilian I. The government of the Low Countries thereupon became in fact as well as name the responsibility of Duke Philip.

Maximilian's own inheritance was a ramshackle one. The empire over which he nominally ruled covered much of western Europe, from France in the west to Bohemia and Hungary in the east; its southern boundary was, in practice, the Alps, and its northern one the North Sea and the frontier with Denmark. Maximilian hoped to make his authority really effective throughout this vast area, and to create a standing imperial army financed by adequate imperial taxation. But in this he came up against the ambitions of the princes and the cities who were the real rulers of Germany. These valued the weakness of the central authority as the best guarantee of their own independence, and they blocked Maximilian's efforts at reform. They were helped in this by Maximilian's inability to pursue any one policy consistently over a period of time. This was in part the effect of his own volatile personality and of his refusal to match his ambitions to the realities of his political power. But it also sprang from the conflicting pressures upon him. His attempts to build up imperial authority in the Empire were constantly frustrated by the overriding necessity to turn away to deal with the Turkish threat in the east or the French threat in Italy. The really effective states in Europe in the late-fifteenth and early sixteenth century were those in which power was being concentrated in the hands of a single dynasty. In Germany the dynastic rulers were the princes. The Emperor had the glory but little of the power.

IRELAND

For about two hundred years before Henry VII came to the throne France had been the great rival and enemy of England, and Henry, like his predecessors and successors, was crowned king of France as well as king of England. Nevertheless in the opening years of his reign he had little to fear from France, where the guardians of the young King Charles were struggling to maintain royal authority against rebellious nobles. Henry, who had found refuge in France as an exile, had no wish, at this stage, to become involved in European politics except in so far as they affected him directly, and in January 1486 he negotiated a commercial treaty with France. Henry's main preoccupation was the preservation of his throne against Yorkist threats, since the Yorkists were not reconciled by his marriage to Elizabeth of York, daughter of Edward IV, in January 1486. He had already had to deal with Lord Lovell's rising, which collapsed before it could come to anything, but a new conspiracy was afoot in Ireland. Henry was nominally Lord of Ireland, but in fact English rule was confined to the 'Pale', a strip of coast some twenty miles wide and fifty miles long, stretching from just south of Dublin northwards to Dundalk. Outside this, the real rulers were the descendants of the Anglo-Norman barons, and the major political motive-force was the family quarrel between the Butlers and the Geraldines. The Earl of Kildare, who was Lord-Deputy of Ireland, was the head of the Geraldines, and had Yorkist sympathies. Henry, however, left him in his post, and contented himself with ordering that the Butlers, who had been outlawed, should be restored to their rights. Kildare's loyalty was tested in 1486 when the Yorkists brought forward Lambert Simnel, the twelve-year-old son of an organ-builder, and presented him—after some doubt about which title to choose—as the Earl of Warwick, nephew of Edward IV. Warwick was in fact still alive, held prisoner by Henry in the Tower of London, but the Geraldines professed to be convinced that Simnel was the true Warwick, and therefore their rightful sovereign, and Kildare crowned him King of Ireland. Troops were raised and two thousand German mercenaries were provided by Margaret, the widow of Charles the Bold, Duke of Burgundy, and the sister of Edward IV. In June 1487 the rebels landed in Lancashire and swiftly advanced towards Newark. Henry, who had had news of their coming and had summoned his nobles to bring their followers to his support, met the Yorkists at Stoke and defeated them in a three-hour battle. The Earl of Lincoln—Richard III's nephew, and named by that king as his successor—and other leaders were killed; Simnel was captured, and started a new career as a turnspit in the royal kitchen.

Although Stoke was a victory for Henry it showed up his weakness as well. The fact that so transparent a pretender had been acclaimed in one of Henry's kingdoms, and had only been defeated after a hard struggle in which half of Henry's forces—either through accident or, more likely, through the half-heartedness of their commanders—had never become engaged, was evidence of Henry's slender hold on the throne and of the strength of the opposition. The attainders that followed, when parliament met, were a sign that Henry recognised his weakness and was determined to deal with it.

BRITTANY

No sooner had Henry defeated a threat at home than he had to deal with one abroad. The struggle of the French nobles against Charles VIII was being supported by the Duke of Brittany, who feared that the increasing power of the French monarchy would lead to the absorption of his own independent duchy. To put an end to this support, a French army invaded Brittany in 1487. This immediately involved Henry VII, for whom an independent Brittany provided a buffer state against France and possible invasion. Henry did not want to become too involved at this particular moment, when his most urgent need was to secure his position after the defeat of the Simnel rising, but he could not ignore the French threat. He therefore offered to act as mediator, and at the same time allowed English volunteers to join in the defence of Brittany. In July 1488, however, the Breton army was defeated, and the duke had to agree that he would not arrange any marriage for his daughter without the consent of the king of France. Three weeks later he was dead, leaving the twelve-year-old Anne as heir to his duchy.

It now seemed certain that Brittany would be taken over for France by a marriage between Anne and Charles VIII, although Anne herself was opposed to the idea and wanted to preserve her independence. Henry was not necessarily committed to war, but the possibility that he might have to fight to save Anne was a real one, and in January 1489 he summoned a Parliament which voted £100,000 for raising an army (see p. 54). He also looked for support abroad, and found it from Spain and from Maximilian. Spain had no direct interest in Brittany, but wanted the return of two border territories, Roussillon and Cerdagne, which had been handed over to France in 1462. She was prepared to join Henry in an attack on France—although her main commitment rested with the struggle against the Moors—but only on terms that were favourable to her. These included the provision that England would go to war simultaneously with Spain, and would not make a separate peace. The acceptance of such terms meant tying English strategy to Spain's, but Henry accepted this risk, and committed himself in the Treaty of Medina del Campo of 1489. He was persuaded to do so not only by the fact that he could hardly take on France single-handed, but also by the clauses in the treaty whereby Spain bound herself not to allow any Yorkist pretenders to take refuge on Spanish soil, and to promote a marriage between Henry's eldest son, Prince Arthur, and Princess Catherine, daughter of Ferdinand and Isabella. This marriage alliance would mark acceptance of the Tudor dynasty by one of the greatest powers in Europe, and would strengthen Henry's prestige not only in his dealings with other countries but also at home.

The Spanish treaty was concluded in March 1489, but in the previous month the treaty of Redon, between England and Brittany, had bound the Duchess Anne to pay the cost of an English expeditionary force of six thousand men, and to hand over Morlaix and Concarneau as guarantees that this obligation would be met. Before the end of April English troops were in action in Brittany, but their success was slight, and although they were joined by a small Spanish force in 1490, this was quickly withdrawn for service against the Moors. As for Maximilian, he was occupied with a revolt in Hungary, and came to terms with France in July 1489. He made a dramatic re-entry into the political, if not the military, scene in the following year, by announcing his marriage to Anne of Brittany. But a proxy marriage was no effective substitute for military action, and meanwhile the French advance into Brittany continued. By December 1491 Anne of Brittany realised that she could hold out no longer, and agreed to marry Charles VIII, thereby uniting her duchy with its mighty neighbour.

Henry was left stranded, still committed to war for a purpose (the defence of Brittany) which could no longer be achieved. Withdrawal at this stage would have been as ignominious as defeat, yet the only alternative was to become even more involved. It seems unlikely that Henry really contemplated a major war against France, but he acted as though he did, no doubt aware that he would get better terms from France by displaying his power than by tamely accepting defeat. He had before him the example of Edward IV, who had conducted a magnificent foray into France, for which parliament had provided the money, and had been rewarded by the Treaty of Picquigny, which guaranteed him a French pension for the rest of his life. Henry accordingly allowed it to be known that he was planning to enforce his claim to the French throne, sent out his agents to collect a benevolence in the summer of 1491, and summoned parliament in the winter to make a more formal and legitimate grant. In October 1492 he crossed the Channel at the head of an army of 26,000 men, having waited until near the end of the campaigning season so that if he were forced to fight it could not be for long. His strategy was successful. Charles VIII had ambitions of his own, which involved sending a French army to Italy, and did not want to waste time, men and money on the relief of Boulogne, which Henry had besieged. A month after Henry had landed, the treaty of Etaples was concluded between the two monarchs. Henry did not abandon his claim to the French throne, but he agreed to withdraw his army in return for a promise that no French aid would be forthcoming for Yorkist pretenders, and that he, like Edward IV, should become a French pensioner. Henry could hardly claim a glorious victory. He had originally entered the war to preserve Brittany, and Brittany had been lost. But he had at least gained a Spanish alliance and added to his revenues. Defeat was acceptable if it made a profit.

PERKIN WARBECK

The provision about Yorkist pretenders in the treaty of Etaples was no mere form of words, for another pretender had already appeared on the scene. This was Perkin Warbeck, the son of a Tournai customs officer, who became apprenticed to a merchant and went with him to Cork, in Ireland. There he was spotted by a group of Yorkist conspirators, who thought that this handsome young man might serve their purposes. Perkin needed a lot of persuading, and refused to pose as Earl of Warwick, which was the original suggestion. He did agree, eventually, to impersonate Richard, Duke of York, one of the two children of Edward IV, who had 'disappeared' in the Tower—officially declared by Henry VII to have been murdered by order of Richard III. The King of France, then at war with England, welcomed Perkin to his court until peace was signed at Etaples. Then the pretender made his way to the Netherlands, where Margaret of Burgundy, whose devotion to her family cause never faltered, not only welcomed him but declared she recognised him as her long-lost nephew. She might conceivably have been restrained by Maximilian, but he was angry with Henry VII who, he chose to believe, had 'deserted' him by making a separate peace with France.

Henry could not do anything really effective to dislodge Perkin from the Netherlands, although he imposed an embargo on Anglo-Flemish trade in 1493, but he acted firmly against possible centres of rebellion nearer home. Lord Fitzwalter and other Yorkist conspirators were arrested and executed in 1494, and were followed to the block in the next year by Sir William Stanley. As for Ireland, Henry had already sent an army there in 1491, and in 1492 he dismissed Kildare—who had now recognised two pretenders—from his office of Lord Deputy. Kildare made his way to England, where he impressed Henry and was reconciled with him after a promise of good behaviour. The king could now recall his troops from Ireland, but reports soon reached him of new intrigues, in which Kildare was involved, and he could not afford to ignore these for fear that Perkin should return to Ireland. He decided, therefore, on a radically different approach to the Irish problem. Instead of ruling through the established Irish families, he appointed his baby son, Prince Henry, as Lieutenant of Ireland, and made Sir Edward Poynings his deputy. Poynings was given an army with which to enforce the king's will in Ireland, and was accompanied by a number of other English officials, including financial ones. The king was clearly planning to bring Ireland under the same sort of household administration that was working so effectively in England.

Poynings was successful in restoring order, both by direct military action and by bribing the chieftains, and to make sure that no future Irish parliament should give a pretender the degree of support that Lambert Simnel had received, he summoned this body to meet in December 1494, and presented it with the draft of a statute which was to become known as Poynings' Law. By this Act it was made illegal for an Irish Parliament to meet or to pass any Act without the prior approval of the English government. The operation of English laws was also extended to Ireland, liveried retainers were forbidden, the authority of the Deputy was strengthened, and—insofar as this could be done merely by legislative enactment—Ireland was brought under the close control of the king and his Council.

The following year Henry sent out one of his household officials, Henry Wyatt, to enquire into the estate of the public finances in Ireland. But if the king hoped that he would be able to make Ireland profitable, or even pay for itself, he was disappointed. Wyatt's figures made it clear that Ireland could not even pay for the upkeep of its permanent garrison, let alone expeditionary forces like that of Poynings. If Henry was to transform his legal sovereignty into an actual one, he would have to spend a great deal of money, and this he was not prepared to do. He left Poynings in Ireland for the time being (although he cut his army to little over 600 men), since there was still a threat that Warbeck might reappear. This threat materialised in 1495, when the pretender landed in Ireland, was joined by the Earl of Desmond and other malcontents, and besieged Waterford, the second most important town in the country. But Waterford, with help from Poynings, defied the besiegers, and Warbeck, abandoning his attempt in August of that year, sailed away to Scotland. By the end of the year Ireland had been pacified, and Poynings returned to England. Henry, who needed money and men for operations against Scotland, now disentangled himself from his Irish involvement and returned to the practice of ruling through the Irish magnates. He had been impressed by Kildare, and when it was pointed out to him that 'All England cannot rule yonder gentleman', he replied 'No? Then he is mete to rule all Ireland!' Kildare was therefore reinstated as Deputy, and—having apparently decided to accept the fact of Tudor rule and to abandon Yorkist intrigues—gradually came to terms with the greater Irish chieftains and secured their submission. By the end of 1496 Ireland was no longer a major problem to Henry.

The storm-centre shifted, with Warbeck, to Scotland. When Henry had been an exile, relations between him and James III of Scotland had been good, and it is possible that Scottish troops were among those which fought for Henry at Bosworth. But in 1488 James III was overthrown and killed in a rebellion, and his son became king as James IV. Henry quickly concluded a three-year truce with the new king, in October 1488, but in the following year he took the precautionary measure of appointing the Earl of Surrey to command the border marches, under the nominal wardenship of Prince Arthur. The three-year truce was extended into a seven-year one in 1493, but these paper agreements were not worth much. The Scottish king, and a section, at any rate, of the Scottish nobility, were only waiting for a good opportunity to renew the struggle against England.

This opportunity seemed to have come in 1495, when Warbeck landed in Scotland after his abortive attempt to raise Ireland. James entertained Warbeck regally and gave him Lady Catherine Gordon, a distant cousin of the Scottish king, to marry. He also set on foot preparations for an invasion of England. But when the attempt was made at last, in September 1496, it was a fiasco. Although Warbeck called on the northern counties of England to rise against the 'usurper' Henry, there was no response, and as soon as the Scots troops heard that English forces were moving against them they retreated across the border.

Although the invasion had come to nothing, Henry could not ignore the challenge thrown down by Scotland. In October 1496 he summoned a *magnum concilium* which made a grant of money for the prosecution of war against the Scots, and this was confirmed by the parliament of January 1497 which, not content with voting two fifteenths and tenths, added a subsidy 'for their necessary defence against the cruel malice of the Scots'. With this promise of generous sums of money, Henry went ahead with preparations for his campaign, but while his armies were mustering in the north the news came, in June 1497, that the inhabitants of Cornwall had risen in revolt against the levying of taxes for a war which meant nothing to them. Although the rebels were poorly led, they surged through the western counties, and by the middle of June were on the outskirts of London. Lord Daubeny, who was on his way to command the forces in the north, was hastily recalled. He brought with him a large body of troops, leaving the defence of the northern border to local levies. The Cornish rebels camped on Blackheath, hoping from there to strike into the city of London [**doc. 23**]. But the royal army surrounded their encampment, and although the Cornishmen fought bravely they were completely routed. The ringleaders were captured and executed; the rank and file streamed back to Cornwall the way they had come.

The Cornish rebellion showed Henry that he could not afford to become involved in a major war against Scotland any more than Ireland. The climate was, in any case, more suitable for negotiation, since James IV, who had tried to take advantage of the Cornish rising by invading England once again, had been chased back over the border by the Earl of Surrey. He was also under pressure from Spain, which wanted peace between England and Scotland so that Henry would be free to join the Holy League against France. In September 1497, therefore, the truce of Ayton was signed, putting an end to the war between the two countries. Five years later, in 1502, this was extended into a treaty of peace and alliance, to be cemented by a marriage between James and Henry's daughter Margaret. The marriage itself took place the following year, and

Analysis

although the union of the English and Scottish crowns, which it made possible, did not become a reality for another century, it confirmed the agreement of Ayton and kept peace between the two countries for the rest of Henry's reign.

Warbeck had left Scotland before the truce was agreed upon. In July 1497 he landed at Cork, hoping, no doubt, to find Ireland as welcoming as always to Yorkist pretenders. But Kildare kept to his new-found loyalty, and the citizens of Waterford sent some of their ships to catch Warbeck. Their prey had, however, already escaped. Warbeck stayed in Ireland just long enough to make contact with discontented elements in Cornwall, and in September 1497 he left Ireland and sailed to Whitsand Bay. Although Henry had treated the west country with remarkable leniency after the rebellion, discontent still smouldered there, and several thousand men flocked to join Warbeck. The king, however, had received warning from Ireland about the pretender's plans, and Daubeny was on his way west with a royal army. In the event there was no need for a pitched battle. Warbeck was beaten off by the citizens of Exeter as he attempted to take that important town by storm, and when he heard that Daubeny's forces were closing in on him he abandoned his troops and fled to sanctuary at Beaulieu Abbey near Southampton. There he surrendered, and in early October appeared before Henry at Taunton, where he made a full confession of his imposture. Warbeck could hardly have expected merciful treatment at Henry's hands, since he had caused the king more anxiety and expense than any other single person; yet Henry in fact kept him in mild captivity, and only transferred him to the Tower after Warbeck attempted to escape. Warbeck, the false duke, and Warwick, the real earl, were now prisoners together, and more plotting began. This was no more successful than any of Warbeck's earlier ventures, and it irrevocably ended his career. In November 1499 he was found guilty of treason, and hanged at Tyburn. Warwick, as befitted his superior birth, was beheaded on Tower Hill.

THE CLOSING YEARS OF THE REIGN

By the time Warbeck and Warwick were executed, Henry was firmly established on the English throne, and was beginning to enjoy the 'felicity of full coffers' of which Bacon wrote. There was no immediate threat to him, either, from abroad, since France and Spain were struggling for possession of the rich cities of Italy. Spain was anxious to enrol England against France in the Holy League—the sanctity of which came from the fact that the Pope was also a partner—and used her influence not only on Scotland but also on Maximilian, who was persuaded to drop his support of Warbeck, and to consent to the restoration of trade between England and the Netherlands. The *Magnus Intercursus*, which confirmed these terms, was signed in February 1496, and in the following July Henry joined the Holy League. Unlike the other members, he was not bound to take any aggressive action, and he kept on good terms with France. In fact the first brief stage of the struggle between France and Spain for control of Italy was coming to an end. Charles VIII's expedition into the peninsula had been strikingly successful, and had shown how defenceless Italy really was; but he did not plan to stay in Italy indefinitely, and the French conquests were lost as quickly as they had been gained. Charles was planning another expedition, to reassert his power and establish it on a more enduring basis, when he died in April 1498.

The new ruler of France, Louis XII, was determined to take up where his predecessor had left off, although his objective was the duchy of Milan, to which he had an hereditary claim. To free himself for this overriding ambition, he let Henry know that he regarded himself as bound by the provisions of the treaty of Etaples, would be prompt in payment of the pension, and would keep Yorkist pretenders out of his dominions. Henry was in the enviable position of being courted by both sides. The rulers of Spain had signed a treaty of friendship with the new king of France, but they had few illusions about his intentions, and the main aim of their diplomacy was to build up an anti-French alliance. To encourage Henry to join this, or at least to remain uncommitted to France, they allowed the marriage negotiations to go ahead. In August 1497 the betrothal of Arthur and Catherine was formally celebrated in a ceremony at Woodstock, but the princess herself did not arrive in England until the winter of 1501. In November of that year the marriage at last took place, and the future of the Tudor dynasty, as well as its prestige, seemed assured.

This assurance was short-lived, and the problem of the succession, which had dwindled into comparative insignificance, became acute in these closing years of the reign. In April 1502 Prince Arthur died,

D

to be followed a year later by his mother, Queen Elizabeth, who died in childbed. The future of the dynasty now depended upon the life of the king's second son, Prince Henry, who was unmarried, and as if to emphasise the fragility of the Tudor hold on the throne, another Yorkist pretender appeared on the scene. This time it was a genuine one—Edmund de la Pole, Earl of Suffolk, brother to the Earl of Lincoln who had been nominated by Richard III as his heir and had been killed at Stoke. Suffolk escaped abroad in 1501, and Henry's alarm is indicated by the sudden reversal of his policy towards the Hanse, which he feared might otherwise support the pretender. Those suspected of being involved with Suffolk were arrested, many of them were attainted and executed, and in January 1504 parliament passed statutes forbidding unauthorised assemblies and providing heavy penalties for those who let prisoners escape. The atmosphere of these years is recaptured by an informer's report to the Council of a discussion held among 'many great personages' at Calais. They were considering what would happen after Henry's death, and the informant recalled how 'some of them spake of my lord of Buckingham, saying that he was a noble man and would be a royal ruler. Other there were that spake in like wise of your traitor, Edmund de la Pole; but none of them spake of my lord prince'.

The need to secure his dynasty drove Henry to consider not only the marriage of his surviving son, but also the possibilities of another marriage for himself. So far as Prince Henry was concerned, Ferdinand and Isabella were anxious that he should marry Catherine, now a young widow, and this was agreed in principle in 1503. The king's own matrimonial projects depended very much upon the European situation, and this was thrown into confusion by the death of Isabella in November 1504. Ferdinand, her husband, was technically only king of Aragon, and the Castilians had no love for him. Isabella's kingdom of Castile belonged of right to her daughter Joanna, who was married to the Archduke Philip, ruler of the Netherlands and son of the Emperor Maximilian. It looked as though Spain might disintegrate, and that France might take advantage of the consequent confusion to continue her advance not only south into Italy but also north-west into the Netherlands. It was to guard against such a possibility that Henry drew closer to Philip, while at the same time he took care not to antagonise France. To make the Anglo-Burgundian alliance closer, Henry discussed the possibility of marrying Philip's sister, Margaret of Savoy. At the same time, in order to sweeten his relations with France, he held up arrangements for the marriage of Prince Henry to Catherine, and allowed it to be known that a French princess might be a more suitable bride.

This shift in the direction of his diplomacy pushed Henry further and further apart from Ferdinand. The king of Aragon's main concern was to keep the new kingdom of Spain in existence, and the principal threat to this came from Philip, who championed his wife's claim to the Castilian crown and announced that they would shortly be leaving to take possession of her kingdom. Fearing isolation, Ferdinand decided on a rapprochement with France, and this was quickly concluded. In October 1505 Ferdinand married a French princess, and paid Louis a large sum of money in return for French recognition of the Spanish claim to Naples: since Spain was, in fact, already in possession of this kingdom, and Louis's ambitions were directed towards Milan, this was a recognition of the status quo, designed to put an end to the causes of dispute between the two great powers.

In January 1506 Philip and Joanna sailed for Castile, only to be driven by violent storms into Weymouth, and thence to Windsor, where they became Henry's guests [**doc. 26**]. This involuntary visit drew the bonds between England and the Netherlands even closer. Philip agreed to hand over the Earl of Suffolk, and to do what he could to bring about the marriage between Henry and his sister Margaret of Savoy. He also agreed to the *Malus Intercursus*, with its highly favourable terms for English merchants trading in the Netherlands (see p. 70). In return for all these, he was promised English support for his wife's claim to Castile, and English assistance in the event of a French attack on the Netherlands.

The death of Philip in September 1506 brought this diplomatic card-house to the ground. To save what he could of the Netherlands alliance Henry now proposed to marry Philip's widow, Joanna. She was reported—correctly—to be crazed with grief by the death of the husband she had loved so much, but Henry may well have doubted these stories. In any case there could be no doubt that Joanna was capable of bearing children, and this would fulfil one at least of his aims. His proposal came to nothing, however, mainly because Joanna's madness was not feigned and became increasingly obvious as well as increasingly severe. Since Henry's chief concern was still the preservation of the Low Countries against French occupation, he concentrated upon preserving the Netherlands alliance while at the same time improving his relations with France. As far as the Netherlands alliance was concerned, he seemed to have achieved this when in December 1507 Maximilian agreed that his grandson and ward Charles, the son of Philip and Joanna and therefore nominal ruler of the Netherlands, should in due course marry Henry's daughter Mary. Henry also continued to press his own suit with Margaret of Savoy, but her determination was a match for his own, and she made it clear that even the prospect of a crown did not tempt her.

All Henry could offer France was a possible marriage alliance between his son and a French princess, but Louis XII's ambitions were still directed towards Italy. Venice, with its commercial wealth and its dependent territories, was the prize this time, and Louis appreciated that his chances of success would be far greater if he could come to terms with Spain beforehand, rather than risk having to face a Spanish-Venetian combination. French diplomacy was therefore concentrated on the isolation of Venice, and its success was signalled by the formation of the League of Cambrai in December 1508. Louis of France, Ferdinand of Aragon, the Emperor Maximilian and the Archduke Charles of Burgundy were all members of this, along with the Pope. The only conspicuous absentee was Henry VII. This diplomatic isolation, however, suited Henry's purposes, even though he had not deliberately engineered it. The big European powers, obsessed with Italy, wanted peace and friendship with England; there was no immediate threat to the independence of the Netherlands; and as for the destruction of Venetian predominance, this was something for which Henry felt a great deal of sympathy, and he had already encouraged English merchants to be ready to fill the space left by the constriction of Venetian activity.

Henry's foreign policy was not the product of a master-plan, carefully worked out and consistently applied. It was rather the reaction to constantly changing circumstances created by the interaction of the great powers of Europe, among whom England was hardly to be numbered. He did, of course, have certain principles in mind: the protection of his dynasty against Yorkist pretenders, the safeguarding of the independence of the Netherlands, and the promotion of English trade. Beyond this he had no territorial ambitions, nor was he blinded by any expensive visions of martial glory. He never tried to act as the arbiter of Europe, nor as the peacemaker, since he could not hope to hold back France and Spain, and in any case their involvement in Italy kept them from intrigues against England. He took advantage of the circumstances which were presented to him; he made his overriding aim the conservation and accumulation of wealth rather than its dissipation in military ventures; and he tied his dynasty into the ruling houses of Europe. It was a considerable achievement in its own right, and there was justice in Henry's proud claim, which he made to the City in December 1507: 'This our realm is now environed, and, in manner, closed in every side with such mighty princes our good sons, friends, confederates and allies, that by the help of our Lord the same is and shall be perpetually established in rest and peace and wealthy condition.'

Part Three

ASSESSMENT

8 Conclusion

When John Richard Green published his *Short History of the English People* in 1874, he entitled the chapter which dealt with events from 1471 to 1509 'The New Monarchy'. He made his reasons for so doing perfectly clear. English constitutional development, as he saw it, had been progressing very nicely under the Lancastrians, with the liberties of the subject protected and strengthened by an active parliament, a time-honoured system of law with which no mere ruler could interfere, and the beginnings of commercial expansion. All this was brought to an end by the Wars of the Roses, for these did 'far more than ruin one royal house or set up another on the throne. If they did not utterly destroy English freedom, they arrested its progress for more than a hundred years.' The people of England had been reaping the benefits of the struggle against medieval autocracy, and had won their freedom from arbitrary taxation, arbitrary imprisonment and arbitrary legislation. But after the wars had done their destructive work the power of the crown expanded to such an extent that it stifled individual liberty. 'The character of the Monarchy from the time of Edward the Fourth to the time of Elizabeth remains something strange and isolated in our history. It is hard to connect the kingship of the old English, of the Norman, the Angevin, or the Plantagenet Kings, with the kingship of the House of York or of the House of Tudor.'

Green's *Short History* was so influential, and its 'liberal' assumptions so in tune with the presuppositions of his age, that his interpretation gained general acceptance. All that later historians did was to modify some of the details, and in the textbooks, at any rate, 1485 rather than 1471 was taken as the date at which the 'New Monarchy' began. The advantage of making a break at 1485 was that it linked the arrival of a new dynasty on the English throne with the more widespread changes that were transforming European society from 'medieval' to 'modern'. Henry VII coincided with the Renaissance, and his son brought the Reformation to England. By these tokens they were obviously 'new monarchs', far removed in their methods and in their philosophy from their predecessors on the English throne.

The characteristics of this 'New Monarchy', as they were later defined by Pollard and others, were solvency, efficiency, autocratic centralisation, the development of the household at the expense of the older, more 'public', institutions, and the use of 'middle-class' men in place of feudal aristocrats. So far as Henry VII is concerned, his solvency is not in doubt. He left no large cash balance to his heir, but a considerable treasure in plate and jewels, and a long list of debts outstanding. Henry's government was also efficient by the standards of the day, it tended to concentrate power at the centre, and it was autocratic to the extent that it stressed the prerogative of the king, struck down offenders by acts of attainder, and relegated parliament to a subordinate role. It worked through household institutions like the Chamber, rather than the Exchequer, and its chief officials were drawn from the gentry rather than the nobility. In all these ways Henry VII seems to conform to the pattern of a 'new monarch' and the battle of Bosworth can be held to signal the beginning of a new era in English history.

There is, however, another side to the picture. It is true that most medieval monarchs, after the death of William the Conqueror, were insolvent, but so were most of the monarchs who followed Henry VIII. Solvency, then, seems to have been characteristic only of Henry VII, not of the 'New Monarchy' as such. Efficiency is a different matter, since so much here depends upon the meaning applied to the word. There was a determination about Henry VII's government that had been lacking from Henry VI's; but Henry VI was no more 'typically medieval' than Henry II or Edward I, whose determination was never in doubt. Procrastination, deviousness and incapacity were not, in any case, unknown during the reign of Henry VII, and even in the financial administration the absence of systematisation led to overlapping and duplication, with all the inefficiency that these entail.

There are certainly centralising tendencies to be discerned in Henry VII's government, but what strikes a modern observer most about his administration is the way in which power was decentralised rather than concentrated. The facts of geography and poor communications were largely responsible for this. In the absence not only of wireless and telephones but even of good roads, the king simply had to leave a great deal of responsibility to the men on the spot—and this meant in effect the justices of the peace. The Council could advise, encourage and threaten, but the king was dependent in the last resort upon the cooperation of the justices and of the propertied classes in general.

The same is true of the autocratic tendencies of Henry's rule. He may have wished to rule in the 'French manner', and he gave his court a degree of formality which emphasised the mystery and remoteness, as well as the splendour, of kingship. But Henry was never an absolute monarch. He was limited by custom and by law, and although these gave him extensive rights they also protected his subjects. Justice was mainly a matter for the courts of common law; taxation and legislation were primarily the function of parliament; spiritual and moral matters fell within the sphere of the Church. These were boundaries which Henry recognised, and even had he wished to sweep them away he simply did not have the means to do so. He had no police force and no standing army: in time of danger even more than in time of peace he was dependent upon the support of the property-owners.

Henry's development of household administration and his reliance on 'middle-class' men is often put forward as the most novel feature of his rule, but there was little that was 'new' about either of these. Medieval administration had never been confined to the Exchequer and Chancery. As these offices moved out of court, medieval kings made increasing use of household departments to give them the control and the flexibility they needed. This was particularly the case in times of emergency. When, for instance, the magnates took over the outer ring of the administration, hoping thereby to force the king to rule in the way they wished, the king would expand the household offices into national departments. The same development took place when the country was at war and the king needed large sums of money under his immediate control: during the reign of Edward III, for example, the Wardrobe became in effect a national treasury. There was nothing particularly new or modern, then, about Henry's use of the household departments; nor was there in his reliance on the gentry rather than the aristocracy for his govern-ment officials. These were not 'middle-class', and the term itself was unknown. They came from the upper section of English society—the ruling minority, or, to use a more evocative term, the 'political nation'—and were new only in the sense that their families had not previously been prominent in central government. Even those magnate families which regarded central government as exclusively their concern had originally been 'new'. Henry I, to take only one example, had been accused of raising men from the dust to serve him, and it may be accepted as a general rule that the 'new men' whom one king picks to serve him found the aristocratic families which assert a natural and exclusive right to advise his successors.

No ruler of England, not even Oliver Cromwell, started with a *tabula rasa*. Despite the Wars of the Roses the traditions and much of the machinery of government survived, and Henry VII was probably only too thankful to use them. The job of ruling late-medieval England was not an easy one, and institutions which had stood the test of time offered the best chance of doing it. Henry did not have the doubtful advantage of knowing that the Middle Ages were almost over and that his task was to lead his country into a new historical epoch. For him the problems of government were much as they always had been. So were the solutions. All that was needed was to make the existing system work properly.

In this Henry was not so different as is sometimes implied from his fellow monarchs, for in Europe as in England the evidence of the past was just as important—if not more so—as the evidence of the future. This was particularly true where representative assemblies were concerned, for these had come into existence in nearly every country during the Middle Ages, and although the general tendency in the sixteenth century may have been towards absolutism, the popular element in government remained of considerable importance. In France, for instance, where the Estates-General met only rarely and had lost its control over taxation, provincial assemblies continued their meetings and operated as an effective check upon the monarchy. The king was theoretically free to raise as much money as he pleased, but in fact he had to accept the limitation imposed by the degree of public acceptance that he could command. He had royal officials throughout France, but they numbered only 12,000 and could not possibly have held down a hostile population of some 15 million. Nor, for that matter, could the standing army have done so, for it was limited in size and effectiveness and had to be supplemented in times of crisis by aristocratic retainers. France was in some ways a highly centralised monarchy, but the provinces, and especially those territories which had only recently come into possession of the French crown, kept their separate privileges.

customs, taxes and codes of law. An absolute ruler would have ridden roughshod over all these, but Charles VIII and Louis XII worked within the complex pattern they created. The streamlined autocracy for which France was to become famous was the creation of Louis XIV, not of Louis XII.

Although the seventeenth century was to see a pronounced shift towards absolutism in the state systems of Europe, this was not obvious or inevitable in the early sixteenth century. If we look for signs of absolutism they are there. But so also are signs of the older, less autocratic, tradition. In the principalities of Germany representative assemblies were flourishing and had developed their own bureaucracy and permanent committees which gave them greater power, in some ways, than the English parliament. In the government of the Netherlands the States-General and the provincial estates were also of considerable importance, and even in this highly urbanised quarter of Europe, which was farthest removed, economically speaking, from the feudal past, the forces of local particularism were much stronger than those of centralisation.

All European states in the early sixteenth century were the products of continuity as well as change, and this is why statements about 'New Monarchies' are only partial truths. One set of statements about what was 'typical' of the age can be paralleled by an opposite set. Henry VII's reign saw the triumph of the crown, the subordination of parliament, the bringing-to-heel of the feudal nobility, the extension of prerogative law, and the assertion of central control. It also saw the survival of parliament and the increased use of statute, the continuance of the landowners as effective rulers of the localities, the reinvigoration of the ancient common law, and the preservation of privileges and franchises on a scale that no modern ruler would tolerate. The present does not totally destroy the past; it co-exists with it. Had Henry VII been gifted with second sight he might have abolished parliament altogether, replaced common law by prerogative action, and swept away the archaic financial system in favour of one that was really geared to royal needs. But he did none of these things. He used parliament because it could do things that no other existing institution could do, and was amenable to his will; he goaded the common law into life, because whatever its deficiencies it was the best system of law available; and he preserved the financial structure of the state, with all its anomalies, because it commanded at least a measure of acceptance, and could be made to yield enough—and more than enough—for his purposes.

Although Henry has been accused of stretching the bounds of his prerogative beyond the limits which custom and even prudence should have dictated, there is no certainty that this was so. From the beginning of his reign until the end he deliberately exploited the rights of the crown in order to make it once again rich and powerful. It may be that in his later years, when he was securely established on the throne, he acted in a more high-handed fashion and was less tender about the rights and liberties of his subjects. But such judgments are relative, and it can be argued just as convincingly that the real change took place not in Henry's policy but in the attitude towards it of the property-owners. They had been prepared to pay a high price for good order after the breakdown of the late-fifteenth century, but as they came to take more settled conditions for granted they resented the remorseless pressure of the royal administration and complained about its injustice [**doc. 31**]. The property-owners showed themselves throughout the sixteenth and seventeenth centuries most unwilling to finance the operations of government, and thereby drove the crown to take advantage of legal loopholes and archaic privileges. There is no point in trying to distribute praise or blame. Henry VII, as king, was determined to rule and to find enough money to make his rule effective. If, in so doing, he and his servants sometimes acted tyrannically, it has to be borne in mind that failure to act effectively would have meant a return to anarchy. As for the property-owners, by their determination to hold on to what was theirs they crippled government and drove it to the very excesses of which they complained; but at the same time, and by the same determination, they preserved those legal and political liberties which in other countries were being eroded by the power of the state.

Henry VII cannot be neatly fitted into categories of 'new' or 'old', 'modern' or 'medieval'. He successfully founded a new dynasty, but luck played a major part even in this: if Prince Henry had followed his brother Arthur to the grave, the peaceful accession of Henry's eldest daughter Margaret could not have been taken for granted, civil war might well have broken out again, and Henry VII would be remembered, if at all, simply as one more in the succession of late-medieval rulers who tried in vain to restore the strength of the monarchy and with it good order and government.

No ruler, however successful, could hope to eradicate in the space of one reign the evils that afflicted contemporary England. Large bands of retainers were not unknown even in Elizabeth's day; 'bastard feudalism' was positively encouraged by Henry VIII when, for instance, he made the Russells the greatest family in the west country; and as for rioting and turbulence, these remained features of English life for several centuries after Henry VII's death.

Even in the more general context of the shift from 'medieval' to 'modern' Henry VII's reign marks no decisive break, for communities change gradually, and different aspects change at different rates. The supremacy of the Catholic Church, for example, which had been characteristic of the Middle Ages, survived Henry VII by less than one generation; villeinage lingered on into the seventeenth century, as did wardship; King's Bench, Common Pleas and the Court of the Exchequer kept their independent existence until well into the nineteenth century, while grand juries survived into the twentieth. No one would deny today that medieval England has long since vanished, but many of its institutions, in their outward form at any rate, are with us still. The monarchy survives, although its function has been radically altered; so does parliament and the common law. Even the formula used by Queen Elizabeth II to give the royal assent to statutes is the same as that used by Henry VII.

If Henry was, as J. R. Green asserted, a 'new' monarch, he was also an 'old' one, not notably dissimilar in his character and his policies from his predecessors, kings of England. He was, of course, no enemy to novelty. Indeed in 1506, when he was reflecting on mortality and considering the style of the tomb in which he would be consigned to history, he chose as his sculptor Guido Mazzoni of Modena, who produced a design unlike anything that had ever been seen in England. In fact the tomb was not built until after Henry's death, and was carried out not by Mazzoni but by another Italian, Pietro Torrigiano of Florence. In its unconscious symbolism, however, the tomb is an appropriate summary of Henry VII's place in history. The sarcophagus itself, with the recumbent figures of Henry and his wife, is Renaissance in inspiration, and, with its pilasters, its putti, and its classical ornamentation, heralds the arrival in England of the new style that was transforming European art. Around the sarcophagus, however, is an exquisite bronze screen, the work of an English craftsman, Humphrey Walker, who designed it in the traditional late-Gothic, perpendicular style with which he and his fellow artists had long been familiar. To call Henry 'a Renaissance monarch in a late-Gothic setting' is not to tell the whole truth, but at least it comes nearer to it than other, shorter epitaphs.

Part Four

DOCUMENTS

The extracts which follow have been chosen for three reasons: first, because they illustrate some of the themes dealt with in this book; second, because they show what it was like to live in Henry VII's England; and third, because they give some idea of the nature of the sources from which any study of Henry's reign must begin. Within the space available only a small selection has been possible. A much wider choice is to be found in A. F. Pollard *The Reign of Henry VII from Contemporary Sources* (**10**). Material relevant to this reign is also printed in R. H. Tawney and Eileen Power *Tudor Economic Documents* (**13**), in G. R. Elton *The Tudor Constitution* (**5**), and in C. H. Williams *English Historical Documents Vol. V* (**16**).

With the exception of the passages quoted from W. C. Richardson's invaluable study of *Tudor Chamber Administration* (**32**), the following extracts come from eight main sources. First among these in order of importance are the *Statutes of the Realm* (London 1816) and the *Rotuli Parliamentorum* (London 1832), which form the basis for any study of Parliament and statute law in the reign of Henry VII. The workings of prerogative law can best be studied in a third source, *Select Cases in the Council of Henry VII* (**2**), which has a particularly illuminating introduction.

Of the remaining five sources the oldest, in order of composition, is the fourth continuation to *Ingulph's Chronicle of the Abbey of Croyland* (**11**). The Chronicle itself begins in the year 655, but the third continuation, probably written by a monk of Croyland who was a royal Councillor under Edward IV, covers the period from about 1460 to 1486. This is followed by the brief fourth continuation, also probably written by a monk of Croyland, which deals only with the events of the opening year or so of Henry's reign.

The second source is *The Tree of Commonwealth* (**4**), written by Henry VII's minister Edmund Dudley while he was in prison in the Tower of London, awaiting execution, from 1509 until August 1510. This is a work of political philosophy, and is of particular interest since it reveals the mind of the man who was closely associated with the royal administration in Henry's closing years, and was offered up as a scapegoat to the property-owners by Henry VIII, in a bid for popularity at the beginning of a new reign.

Shortly after 1509 Robert Fabian started writing *The Great Chronicle of London* (**6**). Fabian was an alderman of the City, and a sheriff, and the *Chronicle* gives a lively, first-hand account of events great and small.

The *Anglica Historia* of Polydore Vergil (**14**), is the major source for the history of the reign. Polydore Vergil was a native of Urbino and came to England in 1502 in the suite of his Italian patron who had just been appointed Bishop of Hereford. Vergil spent most of the rest of his life in England, and in 1506 he started collecting materials for his History, which he began writing in 1512. Polydore Vergil had the big advantage of knowing most of the people he wrote about. He was on good terms, for instance, with Henry VII, who encouraged him to go ahead with his work, and even when he deals with events that took place before his arrival in England it can be assumed that he consulted those who had been most closely involved.

Polydore Vergil's History of Henry VII's reign was more or less copied by Hall, in his Chronicle, and from Hall it found its way into the fifth—and probably the most famous—of the sources used here. Because of his dependence on Vergil, Bacon is not a primary source. His *History of the Reign of King Henry VII* (**1**) was composed in the months that followed his fall from power in 1621, and is therefore separated by more than a hundred years from the events it describes. In spite of this, however, Bacon's work could hardly be omitted from any study of Henry VII. It is, in the first place, one of the classics of English historical writing, and, quite apart from its own literary merits—which are considerable, would command attention because of the fame of its author. And, secondly, it was Bacon's interpretation which, more than any other, created the 'traditional' picture of Henry VII, and even some of its accepted terminology—it was Bacon, for instance, who coined the terms *Magnus Intercursus* and *Malus Intercursus* for the commercial treaties of 1496 and 1506. Bacon's account, in short, is a major source for the historiography, if not the history, of Henry VII's reign.

Spelling and punctuation have been modernised for ease of reading.

document 1

THE DEATH OF RICHARD III, 1485

In this battle was slain king Richard, the Duke of Norfolk, the lord Lovell ... and many others. And incontinently, as it was said, Sir William Stanley—who won the possession of king Richard's helmet with the crown being upon it—came straight to king Henry and set it upon his head, saying, 'Sir, here I make you king of England.''

Thus by great fortune and grace upon the foresaid xxii day of August won this noble prince the possession of this land, and then was he conveyed to Leicester the same night, and there received with all honour and gladness. And Richard, late king, as gloriously as he by the morning departed from that town, so as irreverently was he that afternoon brought into that town; for his body despoiled to the skin, and nought being left about him so much as would cover his privy member, he was trussed behind a pursuivant called Norroy, as an hog or another vile beast, and so, all besprung with mire and filth, was brought to a church in Leicester for all men to wonder upon, and there lastly irreverently buried.

From *The Great Chronicle*, (**6**), p. 238.

EXCHEQUER REFORMS

(proposed by John Russell, Bishop of Lincoln, and Chancellor of the Exchequer temp. Richard III).

First, that all the king's officers of his court of Exchequer use and execute hasty process against all manner persons accountable, and others, being the king's debtors, as the case shall require: and also to hear and determine accounts of the same, and the issues, profits and revenues coming thereof to be levied and paid into the king's receipt without delay.

Also that no person accountable, nor other person being in debt to the king, have any respite, stalment or favour in the said court, whereby the king's duties may be delayed over the space of iiii months next after the time that any such person oweth to yield his account or oweth to pay his debt, whatsoever it be. For it hath been said that many divers officers accountable have been respited of their accounts from year to year, and also of their payments by space of many years, to the king's great hurt, in times past.

Also that no officers having office in the said court of the exchequer have or occupy any office in the receipt.

Quoted by Richardson, (32), p 12.

document 3

THE SWEATING SICKNESS 1485

In the same year, immediately after Henry's landing in the island, a new kind of disease swept the whole country; it was a baleful affliction and one which no previous age had experienced. A sudden deadly sweating attacked the body and at the same time head and stomach were in pain from the violence of the fever. When seized by the disease, some were unable to bear the heat and (if in bed) removed the bedclothes or (if clothed) undressed themselves; others slaked their thirst with cold drinks; yet others endured the heat and the stench (for the perspiration stank foully) and by adding more bed-clothes provoked more sweating. But all alike died, either as soon as the fever began or not long after, so that of all the persons infected scarcely one in a hundred escaped death. And those who survived twenty-four hours after the sweating ended (for this was the period when the fever raged) were not then free of it, since they continually relapsed and many thereafter perished. Finally, however, the disease itself revealed a remedy. For some who sweated once, when they subsequently endured the sweating again, observed the things which had alleviated the first attack, and made use of them as a remedy, each time adding something useful to the cure. Hence those who fell victims a third time to the disease learnt how to cure themselves and easily escaped the virulence of the fever by profiting from their previous observations. As a result it came about (after, it is true, a disastrous loss of life) that an effective remedy was evolved for all, which is as follows. Anyone who is attacked by the sweating by day should retire to bed, dressed just as he is; if the perspiration begins at night while he lies in bed, he should lie quietly and not move from it, for exactly twenty-four hours. Meanwhile he should add more bedclothes, not thereby to provoke the fever, but so that he should perspire gently and naturally. He should take nothing to eat if he can suffer hunger for so long, but may drink enough of his usual drink warmed to quench his thirst. In this treatment care should chiefly be taken not to allow even an arm to be exposed for coolness outside the bedclothes, for this is fatal.

From Polydore Vergil, (**14**), pp. 7–9.

THE YEOMEN OF THE GUARD

Henry, moreover, was the first English king to appoint retainers, to the number of about two hundred, to be a bodyguard: these he incorporated in his household so that they should never leave his side; in this he imitated the French kings so that he might thereafter be better protected from treachery.

From Polydore Vergil, (**14**), p. 7.

document 5

THE ROYAL TITLE 1485

To the pleasure of almighty God, the wealth, prosperity and surety of this realm of England, to the singular comfort of all the king's subjects of the same, and in avoiding of all ambiguities and questions, be it ordained, established and enacted by authority of this present Parliament that the inheritance of the crowns of the realms of England and of France, with all the preeminence and dignity royal to the same pertaining, and all other seignories to the king belonging beyond the sea, with the appurtenances thereto in any wise due or pertaining, be, rest, remain and abide in the most royal person of our now sovereign lord King Henry the VIIth and in the heirs of his body lawfully coming, perpetually with the grace of God so to endure, and in none other.

From *The Statutes of the Realm*, vol. 2, p. 499.

THE SPEAKER'S PETITION FOR PRIVILEGE IN 1485

That everything to be proferred and declared in the aforesaid Parliament in the name of the said Commons, he might proffer and declare under such protestation that if he should have declared anything enjoined on him by his fellows otherwise than they had agreed, or with any addition or omission, that then what he had so declared might be corrected and emended by his fellows; and that his protestation to this effect might be entered on the roll of the aforesaid Parliament.

From *Rotuli Parliamentorum*, vol. 6, p. 268.

document 7

OPPOSITION IN HENRY'S FIRST PARLIAMENT

After the coronation of king Henry had been solemnly per-
formed on the day above-mentioned, a Parliament was held
at Westminster, on which so many matters were treated of (I
wish I could say 'all *ably* treated of'), that the compendious
nature of this narrative cannot aspire to comprise an account
of the whole of them. Among other things, proscriptions, or, as
they are more commonly called, 'attainders', were voted
against thirty persons; a step which, though bespeaking far
greater moderation than was ever witnessed under similar
circumstances in the time of king Richard or king Edward,
was not taken without considerable discussion, or, indeed, to
speak more truly, considerable censure, of the measures so
adopted.

From *Ingulph's Chronicle*, 4th continuation (**11**), p. 511.

A GRANT OF TUNNAGE AND POUNDAGE 1485

To the worship of God. We, your poor Commons, by your high commandment come to this your present Parliament assembled, grant by this present indenture to you, our sovereign lord, for the defence of this your said realm, and in especial for the safeguard and keeping of the sea, a subsidy called Tonnage, to be taken in manner and form following: that is to say, iiis. of every Ton of wine coming into this your said realm, and of every Ton of sweet wine coming into the same your realm; by every merchant alien, as well by the merchants of Hanse and of Almain as of any other merchant aliens, iiis. over the said iiis. afore granted: to have and to perceive yearly the said subsidy, from the first day of this present Parliament, for term of your life natural. And over that, we your said Commons, by the assent aforesaid, grant to you, our said sovereign lord, for the safeguard and keeping of the sea, another subsidy called Poundage . . .

From *Rotuli Parliamentorum*, vol. 6, pp. 268-9.

A NAVIGATION ACT 1485

AN ACT AGAINST BRINGING IN OF GASCON WINE EXCEPT IN ENGLISH, IRISH OR WELSHMEN'S SHIPS (1. Henry VII, Cap. VIII).

To the right wise and discreet Commons in this present Parliament assembled. Please it your great wisdoms to call to your remembrance of the great minishing and decay that hath been now of late time of the navy within this realm of England, and idleness of the mariners within the same, by the which this noble realm within short process of time, without reformation be had therein, shall not be of ability and power to defend itself. Wherefore please it your great wisdoms to pray the king our sovereign lord that he, by the advice of his lords spiritual and temporal, and of you his Commons, in this present Parliament assembled, and by authority of the same, it be enacted, ordained and established that no manner person of what degree or condition that he be of, buy nor sell within this said realm, Ireland, Wales, Calais or the marches thereof, or Berwick, from the feast of Michaelmas next now coming, any manner wines of the growing of the duchy of Guienne or of Gascony, but such as shall be adventured and brought in an English, Irish or Welshman's ship or ships, and the mariners of the same English, Irish or Welshmen for the more part, or men of Calais or of the marches of the same; and that upon pain of forfeiture of the same wines so bought or sold contrary to this act, the one half of that foreiture to be to the king's grace and that other half to the finder of the forfeiture.

From *The Statutes of the Realm*, vol. 2, p. 502.

A FORCED LOAN 1486

The king sent my lord Treasurer with master Bray and other honourable personages unto the mayor, requiring him and his citizens of a loan of vi thousand marks, wherefore the mayor assembled his brethren and the Common Council upon the Tuesday following. By whose authority was then granted to the king a loan of £2,000, the which for him was shortly levied after, and this was assessed by the fellowships and not by the wards, for the more ease of the poor people. Of the which loan the fellowships of mercers, grocers and drapers lent £ixCxxxvii. vis. The which loan was justly repaid in the year following.

From *The Great Chronicle*, (**6**), p. 240.

document 11

THE 'STAR CHAMBER' ACT 1487

3 Henry VII Cap 1

The king our sovereign lord remembereth how by unlawful maintenances, giving of liveries, signs and tokens, and retainders by indenture, promises, oaths, writing or otherwise; embraceries of his subjects, untrue demeanings of sheriffs in making of panels, and other untrue returns; by taking of money by juries, by great riots and unlawful assemblies; the policy and good rule of this realm is almost subdued. And for the non punishment of this inconvenience, and by occasion of the premises, nothing or little may be found by enquiry, whereby the laws of the land in execution may take little effect, to the increase of murders, robberies, perjuries and unsureties of all men living, and losses of their lands and goods, to the great displeasure of almighty God. Be it therefore ordained, for reformation of the premises, by the authority of this Parliament, that the Chancellor and Treasurer of England for the time being, and Keeper of the king's Privy Seal, or two of them, calling to him a bishop and a temporal lord of the king's most honourable Council, and the two Chief Justices of the King's Bench and Common Pleas for the time being, or other two justices in their absence, upon bill or information put to the said Chancellor, for the king or any other, against any person for any misbehaving afore rehearsed, have authority to call before them by writ or privy seal the said misdoers, and them and other(s) by their discretions, to whom the truth may be known, to examine; and such as they find therein defective, to punish them after their demerits, after the form and effect of statutes thereof made, in like manner and form as they should and ought to be punished if they were thereof convict after the due order of the law.

From *The Statutes of the Realm*, vol. 2, pp. 509–10.

A CASE BROUGHT BEFORE THE COUNCIL

To the most reverend father in God, the Archbishop of Canterbury, Chancellor of England:

Showeth unto your good lordship James Hobart, attorney of the king our sovereign lord, that where one Robert Carvyle of Tilney in the shire of Norfolk, the xxix day of June in the second year of the reign of our sovereign lord the king that now is, was in his own proper soil in Tilney aforesaid, labouring in making hay; there came one Thomas Hunston with one of his servants whose name is unknown, in riotous wise, with force and arms—that is to say with long knives, a staff and a spear—and then and there riotously came out of the highway into the ground of the said Robert and . . . made their assault and beat, wounded and maimed him, and left him almost dead, against the king's laws and peace.

And forasmuch as the said Robert, for the salvation of his life, defended himself with a scythe, which he then had in his hands to mow there with grass, and in the same defence happened with the same scythe to hurt the said Thomas, the same Thomas hath sued appeal of mayhem against the said Robert. In which appeal the said Robert pleaded to trial by jury; and thereupon xii partial men by special labour were empanelled, and by craft and subtle means, and also by great labour and embracery and by means of giving money unto them, were sworn to try the said matter. And by such unlawful occasions they passed judgment against the said Robert and taxed him with damages of C marks, against truth, reason and good conscience. . . . By which occasion the said Robert is so impoverished that he is not of power to sue his lawful remedy, after the course of the common law.

May it please your good and gracious lordship, in eschewing of such open and abominable perjury in time to come, to direct several writs of subpoena as well to the said Thomas as to the said xii men, commanding them by the same to appear before your lordship, my Lord Treasurer and my Lord Privy Seal, or two of you and others, at a certain day, after the effect and form of a statute made in the last Parliament of our said sovereign lord [**doc. 11**], and thereupon to proceed and do in that behalf as well for punishing the said Thomas for the said riot and other misbehavings as all the said persons which so passed judgment, as shall accord with reason and your good discretions and with the force and effect of the said statute and other statutes afore time made. And our blessed Saviour preserve your good and gracious lordship.

From *Select Cases* (**2**), pp. 62–3; modernised.

AN ACT OF ATTAINDER 1491

Forasmuch as Sir Robert Chamberleyn, late of Barking in the shire of Essex, knight, and Richard White, late of Thorpe beside Billingforde in the shire of Norfolk, gentleman, the xxiii day of August, and the said Sir Robert the xvii day of January the vith year of the reign of our sovereign lord the king that now is, at Barking aforesaid traitorously imagined and compassed the death and destruction of our said sovereign lord, and also the subversion of all this realm, then and there traitorously levied war against our said sovereign lord and adhered them traitorously to Charles the French king, ancient enemy to our said sovereign lord and this realm, against their duty and liegance; Be it therefore ordained and enacted by authority of this present Parliament that the said Robert and Richard stand and be attainted of high treason, and forfeit all manors, lands, tenements, rents, reversions and all other hereditaments that they or either of them or any other to their use or to the use of either of them had at any of the said days, of estate of fee simple or fee tail in England or Wales.

From *The Statutes of the Realm*, vol. 2, p. 566.

document 14

A PARLIAMENTARY GRANT 1491

7 Henry VII Cap. XI

To the worship of God: we your Commons, by your high commandment come to this your present Parliament for the shires, cities and burghs of this your noble realm, calling to our remembrance the great continued zeal, love and tenderness which your royal person hath to defend this your realm and all your subjects of the same ... and that ye verily intending, as we understand ... in your most noble person to invade upon your and our ancient enemies with an army royal ... to subdue by the might of God your and our said ancient enemies to the weal of you and prosperity of this your realm; so that your said highness might have therein of us your said Commons loving assistance; for the which we, your said Commons, by the assent of the Lords spiritual and temporal in this your present Parliament assembled, grant by this present indenture to you our sovereign liege lord, for the necessary defence of this your said realm, and us your said true subjects of the same, ii whole xv^{mes} and x^{mes} to be had, paid, taken and levied of the moveable goods, chattels and other things usually to such xv^{mes} and x^{mes} contributory and chargeable within the shires, cities, burghs and towns and other places of this your said realm, in manner and form aforetime used.

From *The Statutes of the Realm*, vol. 2, p. 555.

THE ATTACK UPON THE STEELYARD 1493

About six of the clock in the morning, certain servants of the mercery, with others, went suddenly into the Steelyard, a place where the Easterlings [Hansards] inhabited, and there began to rifle and to spoil such chambers and other houses as they might win into. The Easterlings had work enough to withstand them, and the more because of the number of idle and ill-disposed persons that drew fast unto them. Howbeit, at length the Easterlings shut them without their gates, and held them so closed that none entered but their friends and such as they would. But it was not long after the gates were shut but that the streets and lanes thereabout, which are but narrow, were stuffed full of people. Then was beating and rushing and heaving at the gates to have broken them up. But the Easterlings had so strongly shored and fortified them by help of carpenters, smiths and other Flemings that they had sent for by water into Southwark, that they might not do them any harm. And thus they continued upon two hours before the mayor had any knowledge thereof. About nine of the clock, as the mayor with the sheriffs was going towards the Guildhall to have held court, one met with the mayor at Wood Street end and told him of this business. Wherefore the mayor sent some of his officers back to his place for weapons, and the sherriffs sent iii or iiii of their yeomen to warn all their officers to come in all haste unto Saint Lawrence church in the Jury, whither the mayor went. There he tarried a short while till he was accompanied with xl persons well weaponed or more, and then went through Saint Lawrence lane into Cheap and from thence the next way unto the Steelyard. But when he came unto Dowgate the street was so thick of people that he thought not best to enter that way, but turned into Bush Lane, from whence stretches a narrow lane almost straight down to the Steelyard. So soon as the knowledge of the mayor's coming was told unto such as were most beset about the gate they fled as a flock of sheep. They emptied the place so quickly that the mayor came unto the gate at his pleasure and there took a few without making of any resistance, and sent them as suspect persons unto prison.

From *The Great Chronicle*, (**6**), pp. 248–9.

document 16

AUTO DA FE 1494

Upon the xxviii day of April was an old cankered heretic, weak-minded for age, named Joan Boughton, widow, and mother unto the wife of Sir John Young—which daughter, as some reported, had a great smell of an heretic after the mother —burnt in Smithfield. This woman was iiii score years of age or more, and held viii opinions of heresy which I pass over, for the hearing of them is neither pleasant nor fruitful. She was a disciple of Wyclif, whom she accounted for a saint, and held so fast and firmly viii of his xii opinions that all the doctors of London could not turn her from one of them. When it was told to her that she should be burnt for her obstinacy and false belief, she set nought at their words but defied them, for she said she was so beloved with God and His holy angels that all the fire in London should not hurt her. But on the morrow a bundle of faggots and a few reeds consumed her in a little while; and while she might cry she spake often of God and Our Lady, but no man could cause her to name Jesus, and so she died. But it appeared that she left some of her disciples behind her, for the night following, the more part of the ashes of that fire that she was burnt in were had away and kept for a precious relic in an earthen pot.

From *The Great Chronicle*, (**6**), p. 252.

124

CASES BEFORE THE COUNCIL IN STAR CHAMBER

16 February, 1493

In the case of Doget *v* Lord Fitzwalter, it is decreed by the
king, personally present and speaking with great vehemence
in the presence of his whole Council, that a writ of privy seal
is to be issued to the judges of the Common Pleas commanding
them to postpone and respite the proceedings pending before
them between the aforesaid parties concerning certain articles
(which proceedings were previously instituted by them before
the lord king in his Council and were decided between them
by his majesty) until his majesty shall have issued other orders
by a similar writ to these same judges.

Sir Thomas Worthy and others are ordered to place Robert
Inkarsall and Sibilla his wife in possession, and when they have
been so placed to defend them by the authority of the lord king
and in the name of his majesty, and to cause them to be
defended to the utmost of their power against John Parker and
William Parker and any others whomsoever. Because the said
complainants were riotously and violently disseised by the
defendants themselves. And they are ordered to answer when
called on concerning punishment for rioting, and concerning
damages, costs and the interest of the parties.

It is decreed that a letter be written by the lord king to the
Earl of Surrey, that he himself place John Steward in possession
or cause him to be placed in possession. And that when he has
been placed in possession he cause him to be defended in that
possession in the name of the lord king aforesaid in the case
between John Steward and Lady Agnes Coneas, defendant.

6 May 1494

A decree made in affirmance of an order taken by the mayor
of Plymouth and the commons of the same, for the expulsing
of Nicholas Lowe and Avice, his wife, out of Plymouth, for
their misdemeaning and evil living in keeping of bawdry, night
watching beyond reasonable hours, maintaining and keeping
dicers, carders, hasarders, and other misgoverned and evil

E*   125 disposed people. And Sir John Croker, knight, and his sons and servants, by the same decree ordered not to maintain nor uphold the said persons in the said cause against the said mayor and commons. And for their so doing heretofore ordered to keep the peace upon pain of ccc marks.

From *Select Cases* (**2**), pp. 25–7; modernised.

JUSTICES OF THE PEACE TO CHECK JURY PANELS 1495

AN ACT AGAINST PERJURY, UNLAWFUL MAINTENANCE
AND CORRUPTION IN OFFICERS (11 Henry VII Cap. 25)

The king our sovereign lord, well understanding the heinous
and detestable perjuries daily committed within this realm in
inquests and juries ... to the high displeasure of almighty
God and letting [hindering] of administration and justice; the
which perjury groweth by unlawful retainders, maintenance,
embracing* ... as well of the sheriffs as of other officers,
notwithstanding any laws before this time made for the
punishment of such offenders; Wherefore the king our said
sovereign lord ... willeth and commandeth that all the said
laws be duly put in execution.

And it is ordained by the said authority [of Parliament] that
the justices of the peace within this realm, in any inquests of
office before them or any of them to be taken, admit nor take
any panel of such inquests to be returned afore them, but if
the same panel be first seen before them, and they to reform it
by their discretion if cause be.

From *The Statutes of the Realm*, vol 2, p. 589.

* Maintenance: the use of unlawful means—violence, threats, bribery,
  etc.—to support a person involved in a law suit.
  Embracing: the corrupting of juries.

document 19

There remaineth to this day a report that the King was on a time entertained by the Earl of Oxford, that was his principal servant both for war and peace, nobly and sumptuously at his castle at Henningham. And at the King's going-away, the earl's servants stood in a seemly manner, in their livery coats with cognisances, ranged on both sides, and made the King a lane. The King called the earl to him and said, 'My lord, I have heard much of your hospitality, but I see it is greater than the speech. These handsome gentlemen and yeomen, which I see on both sides of me, are sure your menial servants?' The earl smiled and said, 'It may please your grace, that were not for mine ease. They are most of them my retainers, that are come to do me service at such a time as this, and chiefly to see your grace.' The King started a little, and said, 'By my faith, my lord, I thank you for my good cheer, but I may not endure to have my laws broken in my sight. My attorney must speak with you.' And it is part of the report, that the earl compounded for no less than fifteen thousand marks.

From Bacon, (1), pp. 192–3.

WARDSHIP

November 20, 1495: Grant to William Martyn, esquire, and William Twynyho, esquire, of the keeping of the lands late of John Trenchard, tenant in chief, and after the death of Margaret, widow of the said John, of the lands which she holds in dower; with the wardship and marriage of Thomas Trenchard, his son and heir.

October 3, 1487: Item. received of Richard Harp, receiver-general of the Duchy of Lancaster, for the ward and marriage of Humfrey Hill, £20.

February 26, 1503: Item. to Sir Richard Guilford in full payment of £200 for finding of the ward of Francis Cheyne, £30.

May 10, 1503: Item, received of Sir Reginald Bray for the ward and marriage of the two daughters of ... Lovell of Sussex, £140.

Quoted by Richardson, (**32**), pp. 166–7.

document 21

SIR REGINALD BRAY

From a report made to the Duke of Milan. July 3, 1496

I asked him [Aldo Brandini, a Florentine who had just been to England] about English affairs. He said that the king is rather feared than loved, and this was due to his avarice. I asked who ruled him and had control over him. He said there was only one who can do anything, and he is named Master Bray, who controls the king's treasure. The king is very powerful in money, but if fortune allowed some lord of the blood royal to rise, and he had to take the field, he would fare badly owing to his avarice; his people would abandon him. They would treat him as they did King Richard.

Calendar of State Papers and Manuscripts existing in the Archives and Collections of Milan, vol. 1, ed. Allen B. Hinds. H.M.S.O. 1912, p. 299.

THE KING'S PALACE DESTROYED 1497...

The king this year holding his Christmas at his manor of Shene, upon the night following Saint Thomas the Martyr's Day about ix of the clock began suddenly an huge fire within the king's lodging, and so continued till midnight, by violence whereof much and great part of the old building of that place was burnt, and much more harm done upon curtains and bed hangings of cloth of gold and silk and much other rich apparel, with plate and other manifold jewels as belongeth to a noble court.

...AND REBUILT 1501

This year and about this season, when the king had finished much of his new building at his manor of Shene, and again furnished and repaired that before was perished with fire in the xiiith year of his reign, for consideration touching his gracious pleasure—albeit that according to the common story it was forasmuch as in the time of that hideous and fearful fire many notable and excellent rich jewels and other things of superabundant value were perished by the violence of the said fire—it pleased his grace to command that from that time forth it should be named his manor of Richmond and not Shene.

From *The Great Chronicle*, (**6**), pp. 286, 295.

THE CORNISH RISING 1497

The Cornishmen, who dwell in a part of the island as restricted in area as it is poor in resources, began to claim loudly that they could not bear the weight of tax imposed for the Scottish war. First they accused the king, complaining of the cruelty and malice of his counsellors; then they began openly to get out of hand, threatening death to the authors of the great oppression and making bold to seek them out for punishment. While the people were thus in an uproar, two men out of the dregs of the population, to wit Thomas Flammock, a lawyer, and Michael Joseph, a blacksmith, both daring scoundrels, put themselves at the head of the rebellion. When these two saw that the mob was aroused, they continually proclaimed it to be an infamous crime that the king should, for the purpose of making such a small expedition against the Scots, so grievously oppress with taxes the wretched Cornish, who either cultivated an infertile land or with difficulty sought their livelihood in digging tin (or 'white and black lead') from the bowels of the earth (considerable quantities of this metal being found in the area). But they attributed the blame above all to John Morton archbishop of Canterbury, to Reginald Bray and to many other counsellors. Wherefore they urged the people that, having promptly taken up arms, they should not hesitate to follow their leaders; giving promises that in future no taxes should be paid, and that the people should at their pleasure drag to execution especially those evil counsellors who were plotting the extermination of the poor. Instigated by these arguments the people confirmed the two men as their leaders and undertook to follow wherever they might lead. The leaders, having extolled this popular resolution, made preparations for the march and led the disorderly ranks of the mob towards Wells, on the road to London, where they heard that the king was.

When this news reached the king he was moved by sorrow and anxiety, that at one and the same time he should suddenly be embarrassed by a double attack—that is to say a foreign and a civil war. Since the danger seemed equally threatening from either direction he was for some time uncertain which he should deal with first. In the meantime he learnt that James Touchet lord Audley, with several other noblemen, had made common cause with the Cornish and that they were hastening to London with rapid movement. Realising then that the civil war was already upon him the king decided to turn all his forces against it, so that, having subdued the rebellion, he could the more effectively deal with the Scottish business. Accordingly he recalled Giles Daubeney, who was marching against the Scots with an army, and, having levied fresh troops, he increased Giles's forces. However, lest the Scots should learn that he was preoccupied in dealing with a rebellion of his subjects at that time and be the more bold to raid the English border, he sent Thomas earl of Surrey to the county of Durham, there to gather a band of soldiers with which, together with some of the nobles of the neighbourhood, he could keep back the enemy from the border, until Henry could send back to the north Giles and his army, having repressed the madness of the Cornish (which the king thought would be easily done).

Meanwhile the Cornishmen had left Wells, where they had with acclamation accepted James lord Audley as their chief, and came to Salisbury and then Winchester. Finally they turned their course to Kent in the hopes of carrying the Kentish mob with them. In this, however, they were unsuccessful, the Kentish men not inclining towards a revolution, remembering only too well that their elders had often paid the penalty for similar rashness. This failure so lowered the resolutions of the base Cornish horde, that immediately afterwards a considerable number stole from the column secretly and by night and returned home. But when the leaders of the body realised that the Kentish men would not stir, they assembled their forces and led the whole multitude to a hill about four miles from London, which is called Blackheath in the vernacular: they pitched camp on the level ground which is extensive there and ordered preparations to be made for a battle so that they could either give fight to the king, if he should come against them, or else assault the town. They considered that the king must have been stricken by terror since he had not hitherto opposed their progress, and therefore they did not fear, so full were they of confidence, to attack the town, believing as they did that the king had shut himself up in it.

But the king acted throughout with great prudence. He decided not to go out towards the oncoming mob, but to isolate and suddenly surround them with soldiers in some place where, far from home and tired from the march, the rebels could rely on no reinforcements, and when their ardour was abated and their temerity regretted; as he soon did. In the meantime there was great fear in London. There was a general call to arms, the gates were reinforced, guards and sentinels were everywhere posted, lest by any chance that refuse-heap of men suddenly coming down to spoil the city of its wealth should try to force an entry without effort and danger. But the king at once reduced the panic for, when he learnt that the Cornishmen were ranged on the nearby hill and resolved to fight, he at once sent a large force of archers and cavalry to move round the back of the hill, so that, all ways being barred, the wretched mob should be deprived of all hope of safety. Thereafter, having drawn up his army, the king himself left London and marched to the hill. Giles Daubeney went in front with the vanguard and began to give battle to the rebels. The cowardly and ill-armed mob could not sustain the attack. At the first onslaught and tumult their ranks disintegrated. Then, after the line had collapsed everywhere, all turned tail and some, stricken with terror, sought safety in flight while others, laying down their weapons, gave themselves up. Thus, while many were slain, the number of prisoners was infinitely large. All the leaders were taken together, of whom one, that is to say James lord Audley, was beheaded since he was a member of the nobility. The other two, Thomas Flammock and Michael Joseph the blacksmith, were hanged. The other captives were spared their lives in consideration of their rustic simple-mindedness.

From Polydore Vergil, (**14**), pp. 92–8.

BENEVOLENCES

The king—lest the poorer sort should be burdened with the charge of paying the troops for the war—levied money from the rich only, each contributing to the pay of the troops according to his means. Since it was the responsibility of each individual to contribute a great or a small sum, this type of tax was called a 'benevolence'. Henry in this copied King Edward IV, who first . . . raised money from the people under the name of loving kindness. In this process it could be perceived precisely how much each person cherished the king— something which it had not before been possible to observe— for the man who paid most was presumed to be most dutiful; many none the less secretly grudged their contribution, so that this method of taxation might more appropriately be termed a 'malevolence' rather than a 'benevolence'. However, since no one would have it said he was less dutiful, all competed to pay the required money.

From Polydore Vergil, (**14**), p. 49.

NEW FOUND MEN 1502

This year were brought unto the king iii men taken in the New Found Isle land. These were clothed in beasts' skins and ate raw flesh and spake such speech that no man could understand them, and in their demeanour like to brute beasts, whom the king kept a time after. Of the which, upon ii years passed after, I saw ii of them apparelled after Englishmen, in Westminster Palace, which at that time I could not discern from Englishmen till I was learned what men they were. But as for speech, I heard none of them utter one word.

From *The Great Chronicle*, (**6**), p. 320.

A GREAT STORM 1506

Upon the xvth day of January the southwest wind began to blow with such sternness that it turned over weak houses and trees and passingly stripped the thatch and the tile from houses. The which so continued, little or much, from the said xvth day unto the xxvi day of the said month. And over that fell such plenty of rain that thereof ensued mighty and great floods one after another, to the great hurt of sundry cattle and specially of sheep in sundry countries near unto the city. During which tempest the weathercock of Paul's was lift off the socket and blown the length of the churchyard to an house having the sign of the black eagle, where it fell with such a weight that it broke down a part of the penthouse of the foresaid tenement. And shortly after, by force of the said tempest, the Archduke of Burgundy . . . and other nobles were driven to land in the west country, and there for his safeguard and comfort landed. This said Archduke intended to have sailed into Spain and there to have been crowned as king of that province, by reason of his marriage, and thus was by force of this tempest constrained with a few ships to take land, as above is said, for his safeguard. Whereof the king's grace being informed, anon sent unto him honourable messengers, so that shortly after he was brought to the king's presence unto his castle of Windsor.

From *The Great Chronicle*, (**6**), p. 330.

A MIRACLE 1506

About the end of the month of July a cart laden with stone, by negligence of the carter as he passed through Cheap, one wheel went over the neck of a maid child upon viii years of age. The which lay after as near dead upon v hours after, and then revived and told that the image of Our Lady of Barking Chapel held the cart up from her neck. Wherefore her parents in all reverent wise conveyed her unto the said chapel, and after their oblations made there caused there Te Deum to be sung, in giving to God and His blessed mother laud and praising for that fair miracle.

From *The Great Chronicle*, (**6**), p. 332.

DUDLEY'S ACCOUNT BOOK Sept 1504–May 1508

Item. £20 in money for Robert Marshall to be receiver in Norfolk, Suffolk and Cambridgeshire, as Robert Strange was.

Item. delivered for the grant of the goods and chattels of one John Chauncy, forfeited by reason of an outlawry, £20—viz. ten pounds in ready money and £10 by obligation.

Item. delivered the indenture between the king's grace and Lewes de la ffava concerning the lease of his royal ship called the Regent, and the customs outward and homeward of the said ship, for the which the said Lewes must pay to our said sovereign lord as in the same indenture appeareth for several causes the sum of five thousand and one hundred pounds.

Item. delivered for the Bishop of Lincoln for discharge of a fine of eight hundred marks for his mill and fishweirs upon the river Trent, three hundred pounds—viz. £100 in ready money, and £200 by obligation.

Quoted by Richardson, (**32**), p. 156.

HENRY'S ATTITUDE TO EMPSON AND DUDLEY

Although the king was not unaware that, as a result of this ruthless extortion, there were many who rather feared than loved him, his sole interest was to ensure his safety by supervising all details of government; through which preoccupation he at last so wore out his mind and body that his energies gradually declined, he fell into a state of weakness and from that, not long after, came to his death. Had he been spared to live a little longer it may be believed that he would have established a more moderate manner of conducting all his affairs. For in the year prior to his death, learning that there was widespread complaint concerning the plundering in which the two judges [Empson and Dudley] daily indulged, he is said to have decided to restrain them, to deal more gently with his people and to restore what the two had illegally seized, so that thereafter justice and mercy might flourish throughout his kingdom. But even while he was contemplating this reform death cut him off. When he realised he was not to be allowed to live longer he laid down in his will that all were to be given back such possessions as had been illegally carried off to the treasury by those two most brutal extortioners.

From Polydore Vergil, (**14**), p. 131.

THE EDUCATION OF THE NOBILITY

For be you sure it is not honourable blood and great possession, or rich apparel, that maketh a man honourable, himself being of unhonourable conditions; and the more honourable in blood that he is the more noble in conditions ought he to be, and the more shame and dishonour it is to him to be the contrary. Therefore, you noble men, for the better countenance of your blood in honour, set your children in youth, and that betime, to the learning of virtue and cunning, and at the least bring them up in honour and virtue. For verily I fear me, the noblemen and gentlemen of England be the worst brought up for the most part of any realm of Christendom. And therefore the children of poor men and mean folk are promoted to the promotion and authority that the children of noble blood should have if they were mete therefore.

From *The Tree of Commonwealth*, (4), p. 45.

JUSTICE

And specially in this root of justice let it not be seen that the prince himself, for any cause of his own, enforce or oppress any of his subjects by imprisonment or sinister vexation, by privy seal or letters missives, or otherwise by any of his particular counsellors but to draw them or entreat them by due order of his laws. For though the matter be never so true that they be called for, though their pain or punishment should be sorer by the due order of the law, yet will they murmur and grudge by cause they are called by the way of extraordinary justice. Wherefore the most honourable and sure way for the prince to have his right of his subjects, or to punish them for their offences, shall be by the due order and course of his laws.

From *The Tree of Commonwealth*, (4), p. 36.

A DESCRIPTION OF HENRY VII

His body was slender but well built and strong; his height above the average. His appearance was remarkably attractive and his face was cheerful, especially when speaking; his eyes were small and blue, his teeth few, poor and blackish; his hair was thin and white; his complexion sallow. His spirit was distinguished, wise and prudent; his mind was brave and resolute and never, even at moments of the greatest danger, deserted him. He had a most pertinacious memory. Withal he was not devoid of scholarship. In government he was shrewd and prudent, so that no one dared to get the better of him through deceit or guile. He was gracious and kind and was as attentive to his visitors as he was easy of access. His hospitality was splendidly generous; he was fond of having foreigners at his court and he freely conferred favours on them. But those of his subjects who were indebted to him and who did not pay him due honour or who were generous only with promises, he treated with harsh severity. He well knew how to maintain his royal majesty and all which appertains to kingship at every time and in every place. He was most fortunate in war, although he was constitutionally more inclined to peace than to war. He cherished justice above all things; as a result he vigorously punished violence, manslaughter and every other kind of wickedness whatsoever. Consequently he was greatly regretted on that account by all his subjects, who had been able to conduct their lives peaceably, far removed from the assaults and evil doing of scoundrels. He was the most ardent supporter of our faith, and daily participated with great piety in religious services. To those whom he considered to be worthy priests, he often secretly gave alms so that they should pray for his salvation. He was particularly fond of those Franciscan friars whom they call Observants, for whom he founded many convents, so that with his help their rule should continually flourish in his kingdom. But all these virtues were obscured latterly only by avarice, from which . . . he suffered. This avarice is surely a bad enough vice in a private individual, whom it forever torments; in a monarch indeed it may be considered the worst vice, since it is harmful to everyone, and distorts those qualities of trustfulness, justice and integrity by which the state must be governed.

From Polydore Vergil, (**14**), pp. 145-7.

PENAL STATUTES: A CHANGE OF POLICY
BY HENRY VIII

AN ACT THAT INFORMATIONS UPON PENAL STATUTES SHALL BE
MADE WITHIN THREE YEARS (1. Henry VIII Cap. IV)

Where in times past have been made divers and many acts and
statutes penal ... the great number of which statutes penal
have not been put in execution till now of late, by mean
whereof many and divers good and well disposed persons
ignorant of any such statutes, their heirs and executors, have
been put to great loss of goods, vexation and trouble by action,
information and indictments for offences surmised to be done
contrary to the same statutes many years after the offences
were surmised to be done; upon which delaying of so long
time, much perjury, great trouble, vexation and many inconveniences ensued to great number of the king's subjects.
Wherefore be it enacted ... that all actions and informations
from henceforth to be had, made or taken by any person other
than the king, his heirs or successors, of and upon any such
penal statutes made or to be made, be had, made or taken
within one year next immediately following after the said
offence so made, committed or done.

From *The Statutes of the Realm*, vol. 3, p. 2.

Chronological Summary

1457 Jan 28. Henry born at Pembroke Castle.

1461 Edward IV defeats and deposes Henry VI and claims throne.

1470 Restoration of Henry VI.

1471 Edward IV recovers throne.
Death of Henry VI and Edward, Prince of Wales.
Henry goes into exile in Brittany.

1477 Marriage of Ferdinand, King of Aragon, to Isabella, Queen of Castile.
Death of Charles the Bold, Duke of Burgundy.

1483 Death of Edward IV.
Accession of Richard III.
Probable death of Edward V and his brother Richard, Duke of York.
Buckingham's Rebellion.
Death of Louis XI of France: accession of Charles VIII.

1484 Henry leaves Brittany for France.

1485 August: Henry lands in Milford Haven. Battle of Bosworth.
September: Henry enters London.
October: Coronation.
November: Meeting of first parliament.

1486 Anglo-French commercial treaty.
January: Henry marries Elizabeth of York.
March: Lovell's conspiracy.
September: Birth of Prince Arthur.

1487 France invades Brittany.
Bartholomew Diaz rounds Cape of Good Hope.
May: Simnel crowned in Dublin.
June: Battle of Stoke.
November: Henry's second parliament.

1488 Defeat of Breton army by French.
Death of Duke of Brittany: accession of Anne as duchess.
June: Death of James III of Scotland: accession of James IV
3-year truce between England and Scotland.
July: Anglo-French truce renewed.

1489 Anglo-Portuguese treaty of friendship renewed.
      January: Henry's third parliament.
      February: Treaty of Redon between England and Brittany.
      March: Treaty of Medina del Campo between England and
      Spain.
      April: Assassination of Earl of Northumberland.

1490 Renewal of Anglo-Danish commerical treaty.
      Commercial treaty with Florence.

1491 Henry sends army to Ireland.
      October: Henry's fourth parliament.
      December: Charles VIII marries Anne of Brittany.

1492 Spain conquers Granada.
      Columbus discovers America.
      October: Henry lands in France.
      November: Treaty of Etaples between England and France.

1493 Death of Emperor Frederick III: accession of Maximilian I.
      Philip of Burgundy takes over effective rule of Netherlands.
      Henry imposes embargo on Anglo-Flemish trade.
      Attack on the Steelyard.
      7-year truce between England and Scotland.

1494 September: Charles VIII invades Italy.
      December: Irish Parliament passes Poynings' Law.

1495 February: Sir William Stanley executed.
                  Charles VIII enters Naples.
      March: Formation of Holy League.
      July: Warbeck lands troops at Deal.
      October: Henry's fifth parliament.
      November: Charles VIII leaves Italy.

1496 February: *Magnus Intercursus*.
      July: Henry joins Holy League.
      September: James IV of Scotland and Warbeck invade
      England.
      October: Philip of Burgundy marries Joanna.

1497 Anglo-French treaty of commerce.
      Cabot discovers Newfoundland.
      Vasco da Gama rounds Cape.
      January: Henry's sixth parliament.
      June: Defeat of Cornish rebels.
      September: Warbeck lands in Cornwall, and is captured.
                  Truce of Ayton between England and Scotland.
      December: Destruction by fire of Henry's palace at Sheen.

1498 Vasco da Gama reaches India.
Columbus discovers South American mainland.
April: Death of Charles VIII of France: accession of Louis XII.

1499 Commercial treaty with Riga.
September: Louis XII occupies Milan.
November: Execution of Warbeck and Warwick.

1500 Henry goes to Calais for meeting with Philip of Burgundy.

1501 Flight of Edmund de la Pole, Earl of Suffolk.
November: Marriage of Prince Arthur and Catherine of Aragon.

1502 Anglo-Scottish treaty of peace and alliance.
April: death of Prince Arthur.
July: Treaty between Henry and Maximilian.

1503 Spanish drive out French from Naples.
Work starts on Henry VII Chapel in Westminster Abbey.
February: Death of Elizabeth of York.
August: Marriage of James IV of Scotland to Princess Margaret.

1504 France abandons claims on Naples.
Henry imposes embargo on Anglo-Flemish trade.
January: Henry's seventh and last parliament.
November: Death of Isabella, Queen of Castile.

1506 January: Philip and Joanna in England.
Malus Intercursus.
Surrender of Earl of Suffolk arranged.
September: Death of Philip.

1508 December: League of Cambrai.
Proxy marriage of future Charles V to Princess Mary.

1509 April 21. Death of Henry VII at Richmond Palace.

LANCASTRIANS, YORKISTS AND TUDORS

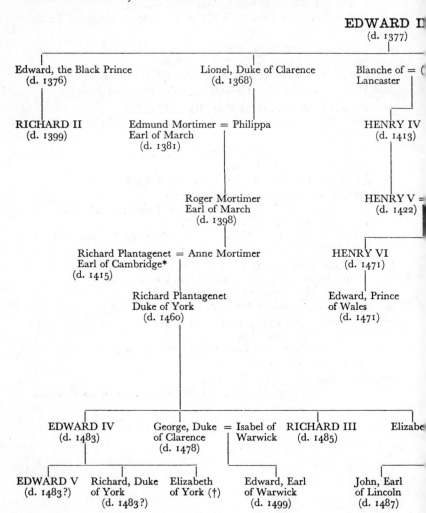

EDWARD I
(d. 1377)

Edward, the Black Prince
(d. 1376)

Lionel, Duke of Clarence
(d. 1368)

Blanche of = (
Lancaster

RICHARD II
(d. 1399)

Edmund Mortimer = Philippa
Earl of March
(d. 1381)

HENRY IV
(d. 1413)

Roger Mortimer
Earl of March
(d. 1398)

HENRY V =
(d. 1422)

Richard Plantagenet = Anne Mortimer
Earl of Cambridge*
(d. 1415)

HENRY VI
(d. 1471)

Richard Plantagenet
Duke of York
(d. 1460)

Edward, Prince
of Wales
(d. 1471)

EDWARD IV
(d. 1483)

George, Duke = Isabel of
of Clarence   Warwick
(d. 1478)

RICHARD III
(d. 1485)

Elizabe

EDWARD V
(d. 1483?)

Richard, Duke
of York
(d. 1483?)

Elizabeth
of York (†)

Edward, Earl
of Warwick
(d. 1499)

John, Earl
of Lincoln
(d. 1487)

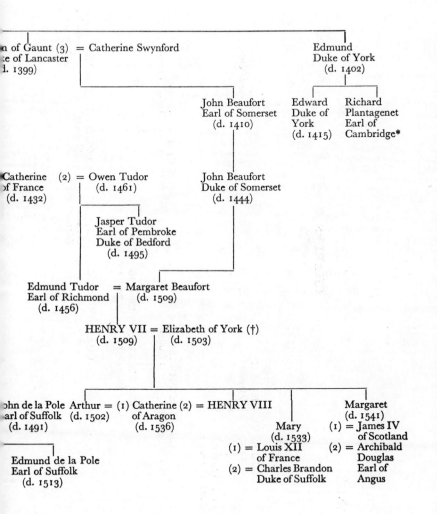

n of Gaunt (3) = Catherine Swynford
ke of Lancaster
d. 1399)

Edmund
Duke of York
(d. 1402)

John Beaufort
Earl of Somerset
(d. 1410)

Edward
Duke of
York
(d. 1415)

Richard
Plantagenet
Earl of
Cambridge*

Catherine (2) = Owen Tudor
of France   (d. 1461)
(d. 1432)

John Beaufort
Duke of Somerset
(d. 1444)

Jasper Tudor
Earl of Pembroke
Duke of Bedford
(d. 1495)

Edmund Tudor = Margaret Beaufort
Earl of Richmond   (d. 1509)
(d. 1456)

HENRY VII = Elizabeth of York (†)
(d. 1509)   (d. 1503)

ohn de la Pole   Arthur = (1) Catherine (2) = HENRY VIII
arl of Suffolk   (d. 1502)   of Aragon
(d. 1491)   (d. 1536)

Mary
(d. 1533)
(1) = Louis XII
of France
(2) = Charles Brandon
Duke of Suffolk

Margaret
(d. 1541)
(1) = James IV
of Scotland
(2) = Archibald
Douglas
Earl of
Angus

Edmund de la Pole
Earl of Suffolk
(d. 1513)

FRANCE

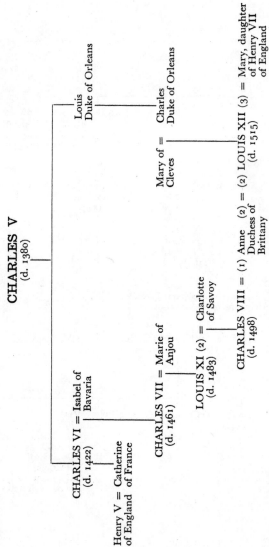

CHARLES V
(d. 1380)

CHARLES VI = Isabel of
(d. 1422)   Bavaria

Henry V = Catherine
of England   of France

CHARLES VII = Marie of
(d. 1461)   Anjou

LOUIS XI (2) = Charlotte
(d. 1483)   of Savoy

CHARLES VIII = (1) Anne (2) = (2) LOUIS XII (3) = Mary, daughter
(d. 1498)   Duchess of   (d. 1515)   of Henry VII
                 Brittany   of England

Louis
Duke of Orleans

Mary of =
Cleves

Charles
Duke of Orleans

SPAIN, THE NETHERLANDS AND THE EMPIRE

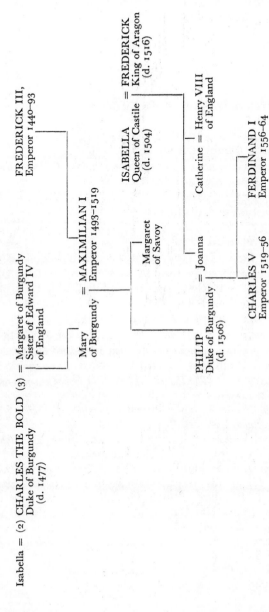

Bibliography

DOCUMENTS AND CONTEMPORARY ACCOUNTS

1   Bacon, Francis *History of the Reign of King Henry VII*, ed. J. Rawson Lumby, Cambridge U.P. 1881.

2   Bayne, C. G. *Select Cases in the Council of Henry VII*, Selden Society, vol. 75, London 1958.

3   *Calendars of Inquisitions Post-Mortem. Henry VII*, 3 vols, H.M.S.O. 1898, 1915 and 1955.

4   Dudley, Edmund *The Tree of Commonwealth*, ed. D. M. Brodie, Cambridge U.P. 1948.

5   Elton, G. R. *The Tudor Constitution*, Cambridge U.P. 1960.

6   Fabian, Robert *The Great Chronicle of London*, ed. A. D. Thomas and I. D. Thornley, London, Guildhall Library 1939.

7   Fortescue, Sir John. *The Governance of England*, ed. Charles Plummer, Oxford U.P. 1885.

8   Lander, J. R. *The Wars of the Roses*, Secker & Warburg 1965.

9   Mancini, Dominic *The Usurpation of Richard III*, ed. and trans. C. A. J. Armstrong, Oxford U.P. 1936.

10   Pollard, A. F. *The Reign of Henry VII from Contemporary Sources*, 3 vols, Longmans 1913-14.

11   Riley, Henry T., ed. and trans. *Ingulph's Chronicle of the Abbey of Croyland*, London 1854.

12   Roper, William 'Life of Sir Thomas More', in *Utopia*, ed. J. Rawson Lumby, Cambridge U.P. 1879.

13   Tawney, R. H. and Power, Eileen *Tudor Economic Documents*, 3 vols, Longmans 1924; new impression 1963.

14   Vergil, Polydore *The Anglica Historia 1485-1537*, ed. and trans. Denys Hay, Camden Series, vol. 74. Royal Historical Society. London 1950.

15   Wedgwood, J. C., ed. *History of Parliament, 1439-1509*, H.M.S.O. 1938.

16   Williams, C. H., ed., *English Historical Documents, Vol. V, 1485-1558*, Eyre & Spottiswoode, 1967.

THE EUROPEAN BACKGROUND

17 Gilmore, Myron P. *The World of Humanism 1453–1517*, Harper 1952.
18 Hay, Denys *The Italian Renaissance in its Historical Background*, Cambridge U.P. 1961.
19 Potter, G. R., ed. *The New Cambridge Modern History: Vol. 1, The Renaissance 1493–1520*, Cambridge U.P. 1961.
20 Slavin, Arthur J., ed. *The 'New Monarchies' and Representative Assemblies: Medieval Constitutionalism or Modern Absolutism?* Boston, Heath 1965 (Problems in European Civilisation Series).

ENGLAND

Books

21 Beresford, M. W. *The Lost Villages of England*, Lutterworth Press 1954.
22 Busch, Wilhelm *England under the Tudors: Vol. 1, King Henry VII*, London 1895.
23 Chrimes, S. B. *Lancastrians, Yorkists and Henry VII*, Macmillan 1964.
24 Conway, Agnes *Henry VII's Relations with Scotland and Ireland 1485–1498*, Cambridge U.P. 1932.
25 Elton, G. R. *The Tudor Revolution in Government*, Cambridge U.P. 1953.
26 Fletcher, Anthony R. *Tudor Rebellions*, Longmans 1968. (Seminar Studies in History).
27 Hoskins, W. G. *The Making of the English Landscape*, Hodder & Stoughton 1955.
28 Jacob, E. F. *The Fifteenth Century*, Oxford U.P. 1961 (Oxford History of England).
29 Mackie, J. D. *The Earlier Tudors*, Oxford U.P. 1952 (Oxford History of England).
30 Ogilvie, Sir Charles *The King's Government and the Common Law 1471–1641*, Blackwell 1958.
31 Pickthorn, Kenneth *Early Tudor Government: Henry VII*, Cambridge U.P. 1934.
32 Richardson, W. C. *Tudor Chamber Administration 1485–1547*, Louisiana State University Press 1952.

Bibliography

33 Storey, R. L. *The End of the House of Lancaster*, Barrie & Rockliff 1966.

34 Thirsk, Joan, ed. *The Agrarian History of England and Wales, Vol. IV, 1500–1640*, Cambridge U.P. 1967.

35 Wernham, R. B. *Before the Armada: the Growth of English Foreign Policy 1485–1588*, Cape 1966.

36 Wilkinson, B. *The Constitutional History of England in the Fifteenth Century*, Longmans 1964.

Articles, Essays and Pamphlets

The following abbreviations are used:

BIHR   Bulletin of the Institute of Historical Research
EHR   English Historical Review
EcHR   Economic History Review
H   History
HJ   Historical Journal
P&P   Past and Present
TRHS   Transactions of the Royal Historical Society.

37 Brodie, D. M. 'Edmund Dudley, Minister of Henry VII', *TRHS* 15 (4th Series) 1932.

38 Brooks, F. W. *The Council of the North*, Historical Association Pamphlet G.25; rev. edn 1966.

39 Cooper, J. P. 'Henry VII's Last Years Reconsidered, *HJ* 2, 1959.

40 —— 'A Revolution in Tudor History?', *P&P* 26, 1963.

41 Elton, G. R. 'Henry VII. Rapacity and Remorse', *HJ* 1, 1958.

42 —— 'Henry VII. A Restatement', *HJ* 4, 1961.

43 —— 'State Planning in Early-Tudor England', *EcHR* 13, 1960/61.

44 —— 'Why the History of the Early Tudor Council remains unwritten', in *Annali della Fondazione Italiana per la Storia Amministrativa*, 1964.

45 —— 'The Tudor Revolution. A Reply', *P&P* 29, 1964.

46 —— 'A Revolution in Tudor History?', *P&P* 32, 1965.

47 Harriss, G. L. 'Aids, Loans & Benevolences', *HJ* 6, 1963.

48 —— & Williams, Penry 'A Revolution in Tudor History?', *P&P* 25, 1963.

49 —— —— 'A Revolution in Tudor History?', *P&P* 31, 1965.

50 Hay, Denys 'Late Medieval–Early Modern', *BIHR* 24, 1951.

51   Hexter, J. H. 'The Myth of the Middle Class in Tudor England', in *Reappraisals in History*, Longmans 1961.

52   James, M. E. *Change and Continuity in the Tudor North*. Borthwick Papers No. 27. York, St Anthony's Press 1965.

53   —— *A Tudor Magnate and the Tudor State*. Borthwick Papers No. 30. York, St Anthony's Press 1966.

54   Lander, J. R. 'Edward IV. The Modern Legend and a Revision', *H* 41, 1956.

55   —— 'The Yorkist Council & Administration', *EHR* 73, 1958.

56   —— 'The Council 1461–85', *BIHR* 32, 1959.

57   —— 'Attainder & Forfeiture 1453–1509', *HJ* 4, 1961.

58   Lord, Robert Howard 'The Parliaments of the Middle Ages and the Early Modern Period', Catholic Hist. Rev. 16, 1930.

59   Ramsey, Peter 'Overseas Trade in the Reign of Henry VII: the Evidence of the Customs Accounts', *EcHR* 6, 1963.

60   Richardson, W. C. 'Surveyor of the King's Prerogative', *EHR* 56, 1941.

61   Richmond, C. F., 'English Naval Power in the Fifteenth Century', *H* 52, 1967.

62   Somerville, R. 'Henry VII's Council Learned in the Law' *EHR* 54, 1939.

63   Wolffe, B. P. 'The Management of English Royal Estates under the Yorkist Kings', *EHR* 71, 1956.

64   —— 'Henry VII's Land Revenues and Chamber Finance', *EHR* 79, 1964.

65   —— *Yorkist and Early Tudor Government* 1461–1509, Historical Association, 1966 (Aids for Teachers Series No. 12).

Index

Absolutism, signs of in
Western Europe 101

Acts of Parliament
Attainder 15, 23, 49, 59,
60, 81, 90, 98, 121
1485 1 Henry VII
King's Title 59, 112
Cap. 7 Unlawful
hunting 60
Cap. 8 Navigation Act
62, 71, 75, 116
Appropriation for royal
household 25
1486 Act of Resumption 22
1487 3 Henry VII
Cap. 1 'Star Chamber'
Act 34, 39, 60, 118
Cap. 3 JPs to take bail
44, 60
Cap. 9 Annulling
London ordinances 61
Cap. 11 Aliens not to
export unfinished
cloth 73
Grant of two Fifteenths
and Tenths 54–5
Act of Resumption 23
1489 4 Henry VII
Cap. 10 Navigation
Act 62, 71, 75
Cap. 11 Wool-buying
by alien merchants 67
Cap. 12 Negligence of
JPs 45–6, 61
Cap. 13 Benefit of
Clergy 62–3
Cap. 16 Isle of Wight 65
Cap 19 Depopulation 62
Cap. 23 Export of Coins
73
Acts regulating
Corporations of
Northampton and
Leicester 61
Grant of Subsidy 54–5,
82
Grant of Fifteenth and
Tenth 55

1491 7 Henry VII
Cap. 3 Uniform
Weights and
Measures 61
Cap. 11 Grant of two
Fifteenths and
Tenths 55–6, 83, 122
1495 11 Henry VII
Cap. 1 'De Facto' Act
58–9
Cap. 2 Vagabonds and
Alehouses 45, 62
Cap. 3 JPs to act on
information 44, 60
Cap. 4 Weights and
Measures 53, 61
Cap. 9 Annexation of
Franchise of Tynedale
61
Cap. 10 Arrears of
Benevolence 55–6
Cap. 12 Free writs for
Poor 61
Cap. 21 Property
qualification for
London jurors 61
Cap. 22 Wage rates and
hours of work 62
Cap. 25 JPs to check
jury panels 60, 127
Cap. 62 Appropriation
for royal household 25
1497 12 Henry VII
Cap. 6 Merchant
Adventurers 61, 68
Cap. 12 Grant of two
Fifteenths and Tenths
55, 87
Cap. 13 Grant of
Subsidy 55, 87
1504 19 Henry VII
Cap. 6 Brass and
Pewter 45
Cap. 7 Regulation of
Gilds 61
Cap. 10 Penalties for
Escape of Prisoners 90
Cap. 13 Unauthorised
assemblies 90

Cap. 14 Special juries
for Livery and
Retainer 60, 61
Cap. 23 Confirming
privileges of Hanse 74
Cap. 32 Subsidy in
lieu of feudal aid
55, 57

Aids, feudal 26, 56–7
Anne of Brittany 55, 82–3
Antwerp 68–70
Appropriations 25
Arthur, Prince 43–4, 56,
83, 86, 89, 102
Auditors 15, 29–30
Ayton, Truce of 87–8

Bacon, Francis 21, 70, 107
Bastard Feudalism 5, 35, 10
Beaufort, Lady Margaret
19, 21
Belknap, Sir Edward 30, 3
Benefit of Clergy 38, 62–3
Benevolences 55–6, 83, 135
Bosworth, Battle of 21, 32,
86, 98
Bray, Sir Reginald 24, 29,
34, 36, 43, 117,
129–30, 132
Bristol 68, 73
Brittany 19–20, 71, 75,
82–4
Bureaucratic Government 24

Cabot, John 72–3
Cabot, Sebastian 73
Calais 31, 47, 67, 69–70,
90, 116
Cambrai, League of 92
Catherine of Aragon 83,
89–91
Catherine of France 19
Chamber, King's 15, 23–5,
29, 31, 98
Chancellor, Lord 38, 48, 61
118
Chancery, Court of 38,
45, 65, 99
Charles VIII, King of
France 78, 80, 82–4,
89, 101, 121

Charles, Duke of Burgundy (future Emperor Charles V) 92
Charles the Bold, Duke of Burgundy, 79, 81
Chester, Earldom of 23
Cloth industry 4, 67–70
Columbus 72, 79
Commissions of Array, 27, 47
Commissions of enquiry, 28, 36, 43
Commons, House of 7, 25, 49–53, 59, 115–16, 122
Constables 46
Cornwall 56, 87–8, 132–34
Cornwall, Duchy of 23, 25
Council, Royal 8, 11–14, 32–34, 37–41, 43, 51, 85, 99, 119, 125
Council Committees 34, 60
Council Learned, The 34–7
Courts of Common Law 8, 35, 37–8, 45, 58, 99, 103
Customs 53, 76, 139

Danzig 74
Daubeny, Lord 87–8, 133–4
Denmark 74
Depopulation 4, 64–7
Dudley, Edmund 30, 34–6, 106, 139–42

Edward III 9, 19, 39, 54, 99
Edward IV 10–15, 22, 25, 34, 41–2, 44, 54, 71, 73, 76, 80–1, 83–4, 135
Elizabeth of York 20, 80, 90, 103
Embracery 60, 118, 127
Empson, Sir Richard 30, 33–6, 140
Enclosures 4, 62, 64–7
Engrossing 64–6
Escheat (feudal incident) 26
Exchequer 8, 14–5, 23–4, 29, 31, 54, 98–9, 109

Fabian, Robert 106
Ferdinand, King of Aragon 79, 83, 90–2

Fifteenths and Tenths 54–5 87, 122
Florence 72, 103
Fortescue, Sir John 11, 27
Fox, Richard 32
Frederick III, Emperor 79

Gascony 71, 75, 116
General Surveyors, Court of 29
Gloucester, Humphrey, Duke of 6
Green, John Richard 97, 103

Hanseatic League, The 73–5, 77, 90, 115, 123
Hatteclyffe, William 13
Henry I 100
Henry IV 9, 19
Henry V 9
Henry VI 9, 19, 33, 98
Henry VII
  appearance 21
  attitude to money 22
  autocratic tendencies 99
  Chamber accounts 29
  descent 19
  description 143–4
  Empson and Dudley 140
  exile 20
  financial achievement 31
  Jura Regalia 36
  loans 54
  marriage projects 90–2
  navy 76
  officials 30
  palace 131
  Philip of Burgundy 70
  prerogative 102
  tomb 103–4
  veto 52
Henry VIII 31, 61, 85, 90–1, 102
Heresy 124
Heron, John 29
Holy League, The 87, 89
Holy Roman Empire, The 79–80
Household Administration 24, 99
Hussey, Sir John 30

Iceland 74–5
Incidents, Feudal 26–7, 57
Indentured Retainers 27

Inquests, sworn 28
Inquisitions, post-mortem 28
Ireland 80–1, 84–6, 88, 116
Isabella, Queen of Castile 79, 83, 90
Isle of Wight 65

James III, King of Scotland 86
James IV, King of Scotland, 86–7
Jewels, Keeper of the King's 25
Joanna, wife of Philip of Burgundy 90–1
John of Gaunt 19
Juries 35, 38, 40, 60–1, 118–19, 127
Justices of the Peace 44–7, 60–1, 99, 127

Kildare, Earl of 81, 85, 88
King's Bench, Court of 28, 35, 38–9, 45, 118

Lancaster, Duchy of 15, 23, 25, 34, 129
Lavenham 4, 67
Law, nature of 58, 63, 85, 99
Lincoln, Earl of 32, 42, 81, 90
Livery 5, 39, 60–1, 85, 118
Livery (feudal incident) 26, 35
Loans 54, 56, 117
London 4, 61, 75, 93, 117, 123, 134
Lords, House of 48–9
Louis XI, King of France 78
Louis XII, King of France 89, 91–2, 100
Lovell, Lord 80
Lovell, Thomas 29, 33, 50
Lunacy (feudal incident) 26, 35

Magnates 5–7, 9, 43, 99, 101
Magnum Concilium 49, 56, 87
Maintenance 39–40, 60, 127
Marches, Council in the 44
Margaret, Duchess of Burgundy 81, 84

Index

Margaret, Princess, daughter of Henry VII 56, 87, 102
Margaret of Savoy 91–2
Marriage (feudal incident) 26
Mary of Burgundy 79
Mary, Princess, daughter of Henry VII 92
Maximilian, Emperor 79, 82–4, 89–90, 92
Merchant Adventurers, Company of the 40, 61, 68–70
Middle Class 33, 99
More, Sir Thomas 52, 57
Morton, John 32, 132

Navy 76
Newfoundland 72, 136
'*New Men*' 33, 99
'*New Monarchy*' 97–8, 101–3
North, Council of the 42–4
Northumberland, Earl of 28, 35, 42–3, 55

Outlawry 30
'*Overmighty Subjects*' 13
Oxford, John de Vere, 13th Earl of 21, 32, 128

Pale, The 81
Parliament 14, 48–63, 97, 101, 114, 116, 121–22
Paston family 5–6, 33
Penal Statutes 35, 59, 62, 145
Philip, Duke of Burgundy 69–70, 79, 90–1, 137
Pickthorn, Kenneth 46–7
Pisa 72
Population 3, 66
Poverty 62
Poynings, Sir Edward 33, 85–6
Prerogative, The royal 25–7, 30, 35, 98, 101–2
Prerogative, Surveyor of the King's 30
Privilege of Freedom of Speech 51, 113
Privy Seal 13

Quarter Sessions 44–6

Rates, Book of 76

Relief (feudal incident) 26
Renaissance, The 97, 103–4
Representative Assemblies in sixteenth century 101
Requests, Court of 34, 41–2
Retaining 39–40, 60–1, 85, 103, 118, 127–28
Richard II 9
Richard III 15–6, 20–1, 23, 25, 34, 42, 53, 56, 76, 81, 84, 90, 108
Richardson, Professor W. C. 28
Richmond, Earldom of 23
Riga 74
Rioting 40, 47, 60, 65, 103
Roper, William 52, 57
Russell, John, Bishop of Lincoln 15–6, 27, 109

Sanctuary 38
Secretary, King's 13, 25
Sever, William, Bishop of Carlisle 43
Sheriffs 44–5, 60, 118, 127
Signet, The 13
Simnel, Lambert, 32, 81–2, 85
Southampton 4, 72–3, 88
Southwell, Sir Robert 29
Speaker, The 50, 113
Stanley, Lord 21
Stanley, Sir William 21, 23, 85, 108
Staple, Company of the 31, 40, 47, 67–9
Star Chamber, Council in 34, 38–41, 69, 125–26
Statute Law 57–63, 101
Steelyard, The 72, 123
Stoke, Battle of 10, 81, 90
Subsidies 55–6
Suffolk, Edmund de la Pole, Earl of 74, 90–1
Sunnyff, Thomas 35
Surrey, Thomas Howard, Earl of 32, 43, 86–7, 125, 133
Sweating Sickness 110

Torrigiano, Pietro 103
Treaties with
  1475 France (Picquigny) 83
  1486 Brittany (commercial) 71

1486 France (commercial) 71, 80
1489 Brittany (Redon)
1489 Denmark (commercial) 74
1489 Portugal (friendship) 71
1489 Spain (Medina del Campo) 71, 8
1490 Denmark (commercial) 74
1490 Florence (commercial) 72
1490 Netherlands (*Magnus Intercursus*) 69–70, 89, 107
1492 France (Etaples) 71, 84, 89
1497 France (commercial) 71
1499 Riga (commercial) 74
1502 Scotland (peace and alliance) 87
1506 Netherlands (*Malus Intercursus*) 70, 91, 107
Tunnage and Poundage 53–4, 76, 115

Vagabondage 62, 65
Vaughan, Sir Thomas 15
Venice 72, 92
Vergil, Polydore 35, 106

Wales 44, 116
Walker, Humphrey 103
Warbeck, Perkin 69, 84–9
Wardrobe, King's 25, 99
Wards, Master of 30
Wardship 26–7, 29–30, 35, 129
Warham, William 32
Wars of Roses 3, 9–10, 13, 19–21, 36, 49, 97, 100
Warwick, Earl of 81, 84, 88
Wernham, Professor R. B. 69, 75
Wool 53, 64, 67–70, 72
Worcester, John Tiptoft, Earl of 6
Wyatt, Henry 22, 85

Yeomen of the Guard 47, 111
York 4, 40, 55